Insurgent Women

Insurgent Women

Female Combatants in Civil Wars

Jessica Trisko Darden,
Alexis Henshaw,
and Ora Szekely

GEORGETOWN UNIVERSITY PRESS

The publisher is not responsible for third-party websites or their content. URL links were active at time of publication.

ISBN 978-1-62616-666-0 (paperback)
ISBN 978-1-62616-667-7 (ebook)

Library of Congress Control Number: 2018957517

♾ This book is printed on acid-free paper meeting the requirements of the American National Standard for Permanence in Paper for Printed Library Materials.

20 19   9 8 7 6 5 4 3 2   First printing

Printed in the United States of America.

Cover design by Olivier Ballou.

Contents

v

Preface

Warfare is no longer just a man's game. The study of warfare, including who fights, is not either. As scholars, we were drawn to the many instances of women's participation in war that went seemingly unnoticed within broad theories of civil war. When we looked to our own regions of expertise, we saw women playing an active role in fighting for separatist causes, in insurgencies against central governments with limited reach, and in confronting the so-called Islamic State. This book addresses the presence of women combatants in three discrete civil wars waged in disparate parts of the world. Source materials are translated from Arabic, Russian, Spanish, and Ukrainian originals by the authors. Our shared focus on women's participation in warfighting is what unites us.

We are grateful to the International Studies Association, which saw the value in our work from its inception and provided us with a Catalytic Workshop Grant. Held at American University's School of International Service in May 2016, the workshop brought together a vibrant community of scholars who are researching women and war and allowed us to present early drafts of this book. We thank Ariel Ahram, Mia Bloom, Kanisha Bond, Dara Kay Cohen, Phoebe Donnelly, Jaclyn Fox, Anita Gohdes, Joshua Goldstein, Heidi Hardt, Stefanie von Hlatky, Meredith Loken, Julia MacDonald, Susan Shepler, Megan Stewart, Laura Sjoberg, J. Ann Tickner, and Reed Wood for their participation and insights.

Many others helped shape this book. We thank Irina Larina and Nadezhda Smakhtina for their valuable research assistance on women's participation in the conflict in Ukraine. We are grateful to Maya Arakon and Mukadder Okuyan for their assistance in translating the interviews from Turkish into English for the Kurdish regions chapter. We would also like to thank those who helped organize interviews in Istanbul and Hamburg. Roxanne Krystalli, Rachel Schmidt, Mia Schöb, and Helen Berents provided insights that helped shape the chapter on Colombia. We also benefited from the comments of the manuscript's anonymous reviewers and the Political Violence Research Cluster at American University's School of International Service.

We further wish to acknowledge Peter Feaver and the American Grand Strategy program at Duke University, which provided funding in support of the chapter on Colombia. Funding for the field research for chapter 2 was provided by the Clark University Faculty Development Fund. Thanks are also due to staff at the Colombian Reincorporation and Normalization Agency and the Center for Memory, Peace, and Reconciliation in Bogota. At the American Enterprise Institute, Kevin Reagan provided excellent editorial assistance and Olivier Ballou contributed a stunning cover design and the organizational chart in chapter 2. Jennifer Morretta contributed the map in chapter 2. A big thank you is due to Donald Jacobs of Georgetown University Press for his support and ability to swiftly bring this book to press.

Most important, we thank you—our reader—for recognizing the value in gaining a deeper understanding of the many ways in which women fight for their causes, their nations, and themselves.

Abbreviations

ANNA — Abkhazian Network News Agency
AUC — Autodefensas Unidas de Colombia (United Self-Defense Forces of Colombia)
CeDeMA — Centro de Documentación de los Movimientos Armados (Center for the Documentation of Armed Movements)
CPN-M — Communist Party of Nepal (Maoist)
CRS — Corriente de Renovación Socialista (Socialist Renewal Group)
DDR — disarmament, demobilization, and reintegration
ELN — Ejército de Liberación Nacional (National Liberation Army)
EPL — Ejército Popular de Liberación (Popular Liberation Army)
FARC — Fuerzas Armadas Revolucionarias de Colombia (Revolutionary Armed Forces of Colombia)
HDP — Halkların Demokratik Partisi (People's Democratic Party)
ISIS — Islamic State in Iraq and Syria
KDP — Kurdish Democratic Party
LGBTQ — Lesbian, Gay, Bisexual, Transgender, and Queer
LTTE — Liberation Tigers of Tamil Eelam
M-19 — 19th of April Movement
NATO — North Atlantic Treaty Organization
OUN — Orhanizatsyia Ukrayins'kykh Natsionalistiv (Organization of Ukrainian Nationalists)
PJAK — Partiya Juyana Azad a Kurdistanê (Kurdistan Free Life Party)
PKK — Partiya Karkerên Kurdistanê (Kurdistan Workers Party)

PUK	Patriotic Union of Kurdistan
PYD	Partiya Yekîtiya Demokrat (Democratic Union Party)
SDF	Syrian Defense Forces
UN	United Nations
UNIAN	Ukrainian Information Agency
UPA	Ukrayins'ka Povstans'ka Armiya (Ukrainian Insurgent Army)
YPG	Yekîneyên Parastina Gel (People's Protection Units)
YPJ	Yekîneyên Parastina Jin (Women's Protection Units)

Introduction

Popular representations of war often feature a familiar trope: a husband-father-son hugs and kisses his wife-mother-daughter goodbye as he goes off to fight for his country or cause. Is this idea of war, in which the men are the brave soldiers who go off to fight while the women stay at home to tend the family, accurate? Society's understanding of what it means to be a warfighter is profoundly gendered, as combatants in both civil wars and international conflicts are almost exclusively assumed to be male.[1] But women's participation in armed conflict is in fact profoundly routine. While it is true that the majority of combatants around the world are men, many women contribute to warfighting and take up arms in both state militaries and nonstate armed groups. This book focuses on the latter: insurgent women. In the following chapters we explore women's participation in nonstate armed groups through their experiences fighting in three major asymmetric conflicts: the ongoing civil war in Ukraine; the conflicts in the Kurdish regions of Turkey, Syria, and Iraq; and the civil war in Colombia. In doing so we address three major aspects of women's involvement in insurgent organizations at three different points in the "conflict life cycle": recruitment, participation, and resolution. In other words, we explore why women fight, how women fight, and how women help bring an end to fighting.

Since 1945 most armed conflict has taken an intrastate or extrastate rather than an interstate form. While wars between countries still occur, civil wars and extrastate conflict (that is, wars between states and transnational actors) are now far more common.[2] This sort of warfare is often difficult to measure and define, given that such conflicts typically involve multiple actors over long periods of time.[3] The shift from international warfare to asymmetric conflict and civil war has contributed to the blurring of the boundaries between soldiers and civilians. When participants in a conflict fight not as part of a clearly identified military but with a rebel or guerrilla force whose members (sometimes intentionally) blend in with the civilian population, distinguishing between combatants and civilians is difficult.

This blurring of boundaries has a gendered aspect.[4] For instance, under the Obama administration, the US military counted as combatants and not as civilians all men and boys "of military age" killed in drone strikes in Pakistan regardless of whether or not they were engaged in combat when they were killed.[5] This assumption demonstrates how gender stereotypes cut against both women and men; in such an oversimplified paradigm of war, soldiers and policymakers learn to see young men as enemies by default while at the same time creating a blind spot regarding the role of women in perpetrating violence.[6] An understanding of women's participation is therefore crucial to an understanding of asymmetric conflict itself. As Karen Gottschang Turner observes in her history of women's involvement in the Ho Chi Minh Trail, "Any accounting of the American war in Vietnam that leaves out Vietnamese women tells only half the story."[7]

This reality has received greater acknowledgment in recent years: in policy, in academic research, and under both domestic and international law. With the passage of United Nations (UN) Security Council Resolution 1325 in 2000, the UN formally acknowledged the impact of armed conflict on women. Subsequent UN Security Council resolutions as well as national-level action plans regarding women, peace, and security have examined women's experiences of war and how their needs can be more effectively addressed in peace processes and post-conflict environments. The role of women in armed conflict—already a focus of feminist scholarship—has increasingly become a focal point for research on warfare more broadly; an expanding and robust body of scholarship has considered questions about how women experience war and peace. Nevertheless, we believe that this is an area that merits further research.

It is often difficult to measure precisely the number of female combatants in any given armed group. Insurgent and rebel organizations are generally loath to publish detailed statistics about their troop complements, so assessing both the overall gender breakdown of such organizations and the number of female members who are serving in actual combat positions can be problematic. This is true of state militaries as well, even though they are, generally speaking, more transparent institutions. Even among the NATO countries, where data on troop complements should be readily available, precise statistics on women serving in national militaries prior to 2000 are hard to come by. NATO requested that member states document the roles of women in their armed forces beginning only in 1998; given that at the time women constituted only about 7 percent of all NATO member-country troops, counting servicewomen may have seemed unnecessary.[8] Moreover, definitions of "combat" are hardly universal. For example, despite having a combat exclusion for women serving in the US military (which was partially lifted in January 2013 and eliminated in December 2015), women deployed to Afghanistan were often operating on the front lines.[9] In Iraq as well, women in US Military Police units often entered combat zones despite technically serving in noncombat units.[10]

Today, women serve in frontline combat positions in many national militaries, including several that have been involved in major counterinsurgency operations in Afghanistan (e.g., Canada and Germany) and others that are involved in asymmetric conflict in other contexts (e.g., Israel)—although women's involvement in military operations has varied contextually and from country to country.[11] Similarly, women have participated in armed rebellion in approximately sixty countries since the end of the Cold War.[12]

Women's experiences of war and their roles within nonstate armed groups are far from uniform; indeed, they vary as much as the roles of male combatants, at least in part because of the varied policies that militant groups adopt regarding their female fighters. This book is therefore less interested in explaining the existence of female combatants than in better understanding how they are recruited, how they participate in armed conflict, and how they contribute to conflict resolution and peacebuilding. To do so, we compare the experiences of insurgent women in different organizations and contexts as well their experiences in the same conflict over time (as in the case of the long-running insurgencies in Colombia); in organizations fighting on different sides of the same conflict (as in the ongoing conflict in Ukraine); and in multiple organizations fighting in parallel conflicts in the same region (as in the interconnected conflicts in the Kurdish regions of Turkey, Iraq, and Syria).

Existing Perspectives and Theoretical Gaps

The assumption that "combatant" by default means "male combatant" is present in a great deal of research on armed conflict. Sometimes this is unstated, as in studies of rebel recruitment that proceed from an implicit assumption that most of the recruits in question are men and boys.[13] Other analyses have carried more direct biases, relying on quantitative models that purport to explain the motivations of all rebels while using explanatory variables that are focused exclusively on men, such as male education completion rates.[14] Meanwhile, studies that focus on the experiences of female combatants tend to treat women as a specific and separate category; this is true of studies of women in both state militaries and in nonstate armed groups.[15]

The failure to acknowledge that "combatants" is not necessarily synonymous with "men" stems partly from the difficulty of differentiating between civilians and combatants in complex security environments. Yet even when women are acknowledged to exist, narratives about their participation in conflict also tend to either minimize women's agency or to emphasize their exceptionalism and deviance from accepted gender norms. Laura Sjoberg and Caron Gentry address this tendency to present politically violent women as aberrant, using the framework of "mothers, monsters, or whores"—frames that simultaneously categorize women as transgressive, anomalous, and irrational but never simply as fighters.[16] Examples of these narratives are visible in places like Palestine, where rumor and the trope of the "fallen woman" are used to explain the participation of women in suicide bombings; and in Iraq, where acts of torture committed by US servicewomen at Abu Ghraib prison were linked to these women's allegedly uncontrollable sexual desires.[17] This stigmatization of violent women partially explains why we fail to "see" women combatants as normal or correctly identify their participation in conflict as being as common as it is. It has also arguably contributed to a real shortage of data on their participation in armed conflict.

Nevertheless, a number of recent empirical projects have engaged with the topic of female combatants and collected cross-national data on women in armed conflict, asking both why women fight and why armed nonstate movements choose to recruit them. Alexis Henshaw examines more than seventy armed rebel groups active in the post–Cold War era and finds that women are engaged in the majority of these organizations.[18] While women are most frequently active in support-type roles, about one-third of groups place women in combat roles and approximately one-quarter have women in some type of leadership position. In fact, rebel groups that recruit women as volunteers are more likely to achieve victory against government forces.[19] Jocelyn Viterna's analysis of female combatants in El Salvador finds that women's participation (and particularly the enthusiasm of that participation) is largely dependent on their social networks.[20] Karen Kampwirth finds that women are motivated to join militant groups by the same grievances that mobilize men and that their individual choices of whether or not to join are driven at least in part by personal biographical factors.[21] Mia Bloom finds that women become suicide bombers owing to a constellation of overlapping factors, including both their own preferences and overt manipulation by the organizations that recruit them.[22] In sum, there is a great deal of evidence suggesting that women voluntarily participate in armed conflict for a range of reasons, both personal and political.

Although the research on women's motivations to fight shows a great many parallels between women and their male comrades in arms, this is less true of the scholarship on the organizations with whom they fight. There is, after all, little (if any) scholarship asking why organizations would choose to recruit "male fighters" in addition to or instead of women, but there is a great deal of recent scholarship that has provided a clearer and more nuanced picture of the characteristics shared by those militant groups that do recruit female fighters. Jakana Thomas and Kanisha Bond analyze data on women's participation in over one hundred violent political organizations in Africa since 1950, finding that women are more likely to be active in large organizations, in groups that use terrorist tactics, and in groups that include women's rights as part of their platform.[23] Examining the role of ideology, Reed Wood and Jakana Thomas find that leftist groups are more likely to recruit women, Islamist groups are less likely to do so, and nationalist ideology seems to make little difference.[24] This suggests that women's participation in armed conflict is conditioned not only by their own grievances and experiences but also by the social options available to them, in a way that may be less true for male combatants.

Taken together, the existing scholarship on female combatants in nonstate armed groups raises a number of important questions, which the cases included here help us address. Why do militant groups recruit women in the first place? After all, in many parts of the world (including the Kurdish regions, discussed in chapter 2) social norms have not historically encouraged women's participation in political or military organizations. Is the recruitment of women primarily a response to personnel shortages, as has been alleged in the Ukrainian case (addressed in chapter 1), or are there other factors at work? Is ideology always a salient factor in determining whether or not a militant group will choose to recruit women? Are more egalitarian societies more likely to produce militant groups that recruit women? At least some of the evidence from Ukraine, Colombia, and the Kurdish regions suggests that the answer to this question is "not necessarily."

We also focus on the motives women give as the reason for their participation in armed rebellion. Are female fighters motivated by a search for personal liberation as women? And, if so, are they particularly drawn to movements whose ideologies champion that objective (such as the Colombian armed groups addressed in chapter 3)? We explore the particular roles that women are often understood to play in both symbolic and pragmatic ways and how these relate to whether or not women are placed in combat roles. Finally, what does the end of a conflict mean for female combatants who were involved? We assess how, as a conflict draws to a close, some insurgent women are positioned to play a particularly important role in negotiations and peacebuilding efforts and what it means to have women, rather than men, in that role.

Case Selection and Methodology

The three specific cases we examine were chosen for a number of reasons. First, all three conflicts include at least one nonstate participant that has a significant number of women in its force. Second, each case offers particularly useful insight into a different point in the conflict cycle: women's varied experiences fighting on opposite sides of the Ukrainian conflict allow us to understand the differences in women's mobilization and recruitment; the variation among the Kurdish factions in the number of women fighting in their armed forces provides excellent insight into differences in women's participation in conflict; and women's historical participation in the FARC and other armed groups and their more recent involvement in peace negotiations make Colombia a particularly good case for examining women's involvement in conflict resolution.

These cases are meant to be illustrative and comparative of the experiences of women in asymmetric conflict and civil war; they are not meant to provide either a random sample or a comprehensive description of all female combatants in all contexts. These cases allow us to discuss a range of organizations in three different regions of the world: the Middle East, Eastern Europe, and Latin America. We also engage with three different kinds of conflicts. The conflict in Colombia is among the longest-running in the world, while the ongoing conflict in Ukraine, which began in 2014, is far more recent. At the same time, those two conflicts are located primarily in a single state, while the multiple conflicts in the Kurdish regions, though separate, are nevertheless interconnected. These conflicts also cover a wide ideological range with regard to their various nonstate participants: leftists in Colombia and the Kurdish regions of Syria and Turkey; nationalists in Ukraine and all three Kurdish regions; and far-rightists in Ukraine. This variation allows us to take seriously the role of ideology in shaping women's involvement in armed conflict.

Methodologically, each case in this book draws on a range of data sources. These include original interviews with activist members of Kurdish women's rights organizations in Turkey and former Kurdistan Workers' Party (PKK) members in Germany; archival material on the Colombian conflict; online propaganda, including both written sources and YouTube videos in Russian, Ukrainian, Arabic, and Kurdish; and a range of other materials, such as government data, press reports, and secondary sources. Whenever possible, we try to preserve the authenticity of individuals' voices in our translations of these materials.

There are, of course, limits to our case selection. Geographically, none of our primary cases come from North America, South Asia, East Asia, or Africa. While there is certainly a great deal of variation among the groups examined, all are ideologically secularist. In the concluding chapter we seek to address these gaps by offering insights into how our findings interface with a broader universe of cases including the Salafist organizations Boko Haram, al-Shabaab, and the Islamic State of Iraq and Syria (ISIS). We believe that overall these cases provide a sound basis for an overdue discussion of the roles of insurgent women.

Overview of the Book

Chapter 1 examines the ongoing conflict in Ukraine as a means of exploring variation in what draws women to participate in asymmetric conflicts in the first place—in this case, in support of both the separatist groups in eastern Ukraine and the central government in Kyiv. The narratives that explain why women fight differ substantially across groups. Women who are fighting in support of the Ukrainian state in right-wing or ultranationalist volunteer militias offer an idealistic, almost romantic view of life on the front lines, whereas women in rebel units cling to the idea of self-defense. Emerging from these narratives are two competing views of nationalism that stem from women's lived experiences in post-Soviet Ukraine and deeper cultural differences rooted in earlier conflicts. The evidence suggests that previous findings that link female participation to the egalitarian or "liberatory" nature of an armed group do not apply in the Ukrainian context, in which women actively participate in violent fascist groups. Rather, historical female participation in conflict in Ukraine, combined with competing nationalisms that emerged with the end of the Soviet Union, has created the space for women's current roles in nonstate armed groups.

Chapter 2 focuses on the conflict in the Kurdish regions to examine variation in the scope of women's participation in asymmetric conflicts. It compares the roles of female combatants in the various Kurdish militant groups in Iraq, Syria, and Turkey. The PKK based in Turkey and the Democratic Union Party (PYD) based in Syria both recruit women in large numbers; as much as 40 percent of their fighting forces are estimated to be female.[25] The PKK's units are mixed, while the Syrian Kurdish military forces are split into male People's Protection Units (YPG) and female Women's Protection Units (YPJ). In contrast, the Iraqi Kurdish armed groups—the Patriotic Union of Kurdistan (PUK) and the Kurdish Democratic Party (KDP)—whose armed forces are collectively referred to as the *peshmerga*, have far fewer female fighters. The histories of Kurdish political mobilization in Iraq, Syria, and Turkey, the ideologies of the groups involved, and the processes by which women became involved in the movement help explain this difference.

Chapter 3 uses the examples of the Revolutionary Armed Forces of Colombia (FARC) and the National Liberation Army (ELN) to extend the analysis of women in conflict by examining women's changing roles over time as well as how gender impacts the processes of peacemaking and post-conflict disarmament, demobilization, and reintegration (DDR). Like the PKK in the Middle East, the FARC and the ELN have a high prevalence of women throughout their ranks (estimated at 30 to 40 percent and about 25 percent, respectively), and women have played prominent roles in the negotiating teams of both organizations.[26] The presence of women in the FARC's combat ranks and at the negotiating table was integral to shaping the outcomes reached in the Havana peace process. Women's involvement was particularly important in forging strategic partnerships with negotiators from the government and NGOs, in promoting the inclusion of gender and sexuality issues, and in shaping a post-conflict demobilization program that met the unique needs of female combatants. Additionally, our analysis shows that the ELN has tried to emulate the FARC as it pursues its own peace agreement with the government by deploying women in visible positions on its negotiating team as a signal of commitment to the process.

The concluding chapter briefly examines three additional contemporary cases of nonstate armed actors that recruit women: ISIS, Boko Haram, and al-Shabaab. These cases widen the geographic focus of analysis to include Africa and the ideological focus of analysis to include Salafism. They corroborate many of the findings of the three main cases and also illuminate important differences regarding the treatment of female noncombatants by nonstate armed groups. We also explore the treatment of ex-combatants by their families, governments, and societies. The final chapter concludes with a focus on the policy implications of our analysis and suggestions for the direction of further scholarship. Are there any clear patterns in the recruitment and mobilization of women into nonstate armed groups? What are the implications for future peace processes and DDR efforts in recognizing (or ignoring) the role of insurgent women?

Notes

1. See, for example, Joshua S. Goldstein, *War and Gender: How Gender Shapes the War System and Vice Versa* (Cambridge: Cambridge University Press, 2003); Megan MacKenzie, *Beyond the Band of Brothers: The US Military and the Myth That Women Can't Fight* (Cambridge: Cambridge University Press, 2015); and Cynthia Enloe, *Maneuvers: The International Politics of Militarizing Women's Lives* (Berkeley: University of California Press, 2000).

2. Meredith Reid Sarkees, Frank Whelon Wayman, and J. David Singer, "Inter-State, Intra-State, and Extra-State Wars: A Comprehensive Look at Their Distribution over Time, 1816–1997," *International Studies Quarterly* 47, no. 1 (2003): 49–70, doi:10.1111/1468–2478.4701003.

3. In this book we use a threshold of more than one thousand battle deaths in a year to define an armed conflict, although, in the context of asymmetric conflict, accurately counting casualties can be tremendously difficult. We base this threshold in part on the one used by the Uppsala Conflict Data Program's widely used dataset. See the "Ukraine" entry in Uppsala Conflict Data Program, accessed August 28, 2018, http://www.ucdp.uu.se/#country/369.

4. Megan MacKenzie, "Securitization and Desecuritization: Female Soldiers and the Reconstruction of Women in Post-Conflict Sierra Leone," *Security Studies* 18, no. 2 (2009): 241–61, doi:10.1080/09636410902900061.

5. Jo Becker and Scott Shane, "Secret 'Kill List' Tests Obama's Principles," *New York Times*, May 29, 2012, https://www.nytimes.com/2012/05/29/world /obamas-leadership-in-war-on-al-qaeda.html.

6. On the risks faced by men and boys in conflicts wherein they are presumed to be default combatants see, for example, R. Charli Carpenter, "Recognizing Gender-Based Violence against Civilian Men and Boys in Conflict Situations," *Security Dialogue* 37, no. 1 (2006): 83–103, doi:10.1177/0967010606064139; and Jessica Trisko Darden and Izabela Steflja, "Making Civilian Casualties Count: Approaches to Documenting the Human Cost of War," *Human Rights Review* 14, no. 4 (2013): 347–66, doi:10.1007/s12142-013-0274-2.

7. Karen Gottschang Turner with Phan Thanh Hao, *Even the Women Must Fight: Memories of War from North Vietnam* (New York: John Wiley & Sons, 1998), 19.

8. *2016 Summary of the National Reports of NATO Member and Partner Nations to the NATO Committee on Gender Perspectives* (Brussels: North Atlantic Treaty Organization, 2017), 7–9, https://www.nato.int/nato_static_fl2014/assets /pdf/pdf_2018_01/1801-2016-Summary-NR-to-NCGP.pdf.

9. Gayle Tzemach Lemmon, "Women in Combat? They've Already Been Serving on the Front Lines, with Heroism," *Los Angeles Times*, December 4, 2015, http://www.latimes.com/opinion/op-ed/la-oe-1204-lemmon-women-combat -20151204-story.html; and Alissa J. Rubin, "On the Job in Afghanistan, Female Soldiers Reflect," *New York Times*, January 28, 2013, https://atwar.blogs.nytimes .com/2013/01/28/on-the-job-in-afghanistan-female-soldiers-reflect/.

10. James Dao, "When the Bullets Flew, 'They Didn't Care That I Was a Woman,'" *New York Times*, January 24, 2013, https://www.nytimes.com/2013/01/25 /us/from-front-lines-women-offer-evidence-on-ability-in-combat.html.

11. "Roundup: Israel and Canada Provide Lessons on Women in Combat," *New York Times*, January 25, 2013, https://atwar.blogs.nytimes.com/2013/01/25 /roundup-israel-and-canada-provide-lessons-on-women-in-combat/.

12. Dyan E. Mazurana, "Women, Girls, and Non-State Armed Opposition Groups," in *Women and Wars*, ed. Carol Cohn (Cambridge: Polity Press, 2014), 146–68.

13. These include Scott Gates, "Recruitment and Allegiance: The Microfoundations of Rebellion," *Journal of Conflict Resolution* 46, no. 1 (2002): 111–30, doi :10.1177/0022002702046001007; and Tor G. Jakobsen and Indra De Soysa, "Give Me Liberty, or Give Me Death! State Repression, Ethnic Grievance and Civil War, 1981–2004," *Civil Wars* 11, no. 2 (2009): 137–57, doi:10.1080/13698240802 631061.

14. See Macartan Humphreys and Jeremy M. Weinstein, "Who Fights? The Determinants of Participation in Civil War," *American Journal of Political Science* 52, no. 2 (2008): 436–55, doi:10.1111/j.1540-5907.2008.00322.x.

15. Mia Bloom, *Bombshell: Women and Terrorism* (Philadelphia: University of Pennsylvania Press, 2012); Dara Kay Cohen, "Female Combatants and the Perpetration of Violence: Wartime Rape in the Sierra Leone Civil War," *World Politics* 65, no. 3 (2013): 383–415, doi:10.1017/S0043887113000105; Karen Kampwirth, *Women and Guerrilla Movements: Nicaragua, El Salvador, Chiapas, Cuba* (University Park: Pennsylvania State University Press, 2002); Megan H. MacKenzie, *Female Soldiers in Sierra Leone: Sex, Security, and Post-Conflict Development* (New York: New York University Press, 2012); Jocelyn S. Viterna, "Pulled, Pushed, and Persuaded: Explaining Women's Mobilization into the Salvadoran Guerrilla Army," *American Journal of Sociology* 112, no. 1 (2006): 1–45, doi:10.1086/502690.

16. Laura Sjoberg and Caron E. Gentry, *Mothers, Monsters, Whores: Women's Violence in Global Politics* (London: Zed, 2007).

17. Anat Berko, *The Smarter Bomb: Women and Children as Suicide Bombers* (Lanham, MD: Rowman & Littlefield, 2012), 5; Sjoberg and Gentry, *Mothers, Monsters, Whores*, 64–75.

18. Alexis Leanna Henshaw, "Where Women Rebel: Patterns of Women's Participation," *International Feminist Journal of Politics* 18, no. 1 (2016): 39–60, doi:10.1080/14616742; Alexis Leanna Henshaw, "Why Women Rebel: Greed, Grievance, and Women in Armed Rebel Groups," *Journal of Global Security Studies* 1, no. 3 (2016): 204–19, doi:10.1093/jogss/ogw008.

19. The opposite is true for rebel groups that forcibly recruit women. Alex Braithwaite and Luna B. Ruiz, "Female Combatants, Forced Recruitment, and Civil Conflict Outcomes," *Research and Politics* 5, no. 2 (2018): 1–7, doi:10.1177/2053168018770559.

20. Viterna, "Pulled, Pushed, and Persuaded."

21. Kampwirth, *Women and Guerrilla Movements*.

22. Bloom, *Bombshell*.

23. Jakana L. Thomas and Kanisha Bond, "Women's Participation in Violent Political Organizations," *American Political Science Review* 109, no. 2 (2015): 488–506, doi:10.1017/S0003055415000313.

24. Reed M. Wood and Jakana L. Thomas, "Women on the Frontline: Rebel Group Ideology and Women's Participation in Violent Rebellion," *Journal of Peace Research* 54, no. 1 (2017): 31–46, doi:10.1177/0022343316675025.

25. Haidar Khezri, "Kurdish Troops Fight for Freedom—and Women's Equality—on Battlegrounds across Middle East," *The Conversation*, March 19, 2018, http://theconversation.com/kurdish-troops-fight-for-freedom-and-womens-equality-on-battlegrounds-across-middle-east-91364; "Female Fighting Force of

the PKK," *BBC News*, January 5, 2014, http://www.bbc.com/news/av/world
-middle-east-25610424/who-are-the-female-fighters-of-the-pkk.

26. Jacqueline O'Neill, "Are Women the Key to Peace in Colombia?," *Foreign Policy*, April 21, 2015, https://foreignpolicy.com/2015/04/20/are-women-the-key
-to-peace-in-colombia-farc-talks/; Jamille Bigio, Rachel Vogelstein, and Anne Connell, "Women's Participation in Peace Processes: Colombia," *Council on Foreign Relations* blog, December 15, 2017, https://www.cfr.org/blog/womens
-participation-peace-processes-colombia.

1

Ukraine

Defending the Motherland

> It's offensive that we are fighting and they just abandoned us here. And now it's up to us "weak" girls and the men that are left here to fight. All the others, I don't know what to call them—traitors probably. The only thing is, let the ones who left return and show what they can do and that they are worthy to live on this land.
>
> —"Belka" (Squirrel), separatist fighter

Women are hypervisible in the Ukraine conflict.[1] Media headlines about the conflict exclaim, "In the Donbass [region], war and peace are in the hands of women."[2] The presence of women, particularly as fighters in armed groups, is a key feature of the war's media coverage and propaganda. Within this conflict, however, women's experiences vary significantly among the armed groups in which they participate. Women are engaged in a mix of roles, including domestic tasks, logistical support, and combat. In addition, some women hold prominent political and military leadership roles.

Existing explanations of why women participate in war do not easily map onto women's participation in nonstate armed groups in Ukraine. Few would describe Ukraine as an egalitarian country; multiple measures of gender equality place Ukraine solidly in the middle of the pack internationally, and traditional gender roles hold steadfast. The fact that female combatants and traditional gender hierarchies can coexist in Ukraine is perhaps best illustrated by the fact that not only are beauty pageants held for female fighters, they are also well-publicized.[3] Clearly the erosion of traditional gender roles cannot account for women's involvement in the current conflict. While some of the rebel groups fighting in the eastern regions of Donetsk and Luhansk do espouse a general socialist orientation (largely out of a fondness for the Soviet Union), they do not appear any more committed to an emancipatory project for women than the right-wing nationalist groups supporting Kyiv.

If gender equality and political ideology do not adequately explain women's participation in the conflict in Ukraine, what can account for it? To explain the dynamics of women's participation in the Ukraine conflict (which began in the spring of 2014), we argue that the historical precedent of female participation in political violence during World War II, women's extensive involvement in the Euromaidan protests, and a resurgence of nationalist ideology in recent years have led some women to take on combat roles.

Rather than simply reflecting a manpower shortage, though, the utilization of women as fighters in nonstate armed groups on both sides of the conflict in Ukraine echoes women's roles as active participants in historical conflicts related to the direction of the country itself. Prior to and during the Second World War, Ukrainians self-organized into local militia and insurgent groups to unseat standing political leaders and resist foreign intrusions into Ukrainian territory. Women played an essential role in this process. This historical precedent, combined with competing nationalist narratives, helped create the opportunity for women to participate in the current conflict—even in the absence of other facilitating factors identified in scholarship on the subject.

Both structural conditions and individual-level motivations have contributed to Ukrainian women's mobilization for war. In many ways the variation in women's experiences and participation in the current war in Ukraine stems from individual women's positions relative to long-standing fault lines in Ukrainian society. From the Euromaidan protests of 2013 to Ukrainian independence in 1991 to the years preceding the Second World War, political tensions in Ukraine have often been rooted in competing nationalist narratives. Those fighting on behalf of the Ukrainian central government in Kyiv (including both the Ukrainian national military and volunteer militias) seek to maintain Ukraine's territorial integrity and resist Russian attempts to undermine Ukraine's independence. Those fighting for autonomy or separatism in the eastern regions of Donetsk and Luhansk (collectively referred to as the Donbass) believe that the Ukrainian state has targeted its Russian-speaking minority through education policies that undermine the use of Russian as a language, effectively breaking the post-Soviet social contract. In the separatists' view, they are fighting to preserve their ethnic identity and break the yoke of Kyiv.

This chapter focuses on the variation in women's motivations and participation in nonstate armed groups with distinct ideologies within a single conflict. It begins with a historical overview of women's roles in past conflicts in the region and describes how women's participation has evolved over the course of the current conflict in Ukraine. We examine the roles women are playing in the two main categories of nonstate armed groups (pro-government and separatist) and address some broad themes in their motivations for joining these groups. Traditional arguments about the groups' openness to integrating women—based on their structure or ideological orientation—do not explain the existing patterns of women's mobilization in Ukraine. Instead, permissive structural conditions and individual motivations and circumstances are the primary drivers of women's participation.

Ukrainian Nationalism(s) and Mobilization

Throughout much of its history Ukraine was divided between Russia and other central European powers. In the late 1920s, when parts of what is now Ukraine were under Polish rule, Ukrainian women began participating in oppositional Ukrainian nationalist organizations, the most prominent of which was Orhanizatsyia Ukrayins'kykh Natsionalistiv (Organization of Ukrainian Nationalists), or OUN. While only limited information is available about women's roles during this period, one woman—Olha Berbytska—was tried for the assassination of a Polish school official in 1928.[4] During World War II the OUN coordinated underground activities in Soviet-occupied western Ukraine and operated openly in German-occupied Poland with the hope of creating an independent Ukrainian state. In the early 1940s women also began joining Ukrayins'ka Povstans'ka Armiya (Ukrainian Insurgent Army), the UPA. Participation in both the OUN and the UPA provided an opportunity for women to become involved in the cause of an independent Ukraine, a country they hoped would provide them with full rights and equality. According to Larysa Zariczniak, "even though Ukrainian women were represented as bearers of the Ukrainian nation by the upper echelons of the Organization of Ukrainian Nationalists (OUN), they joined the UPA as individuals and the roles Ukrainian women played in the underground were just as important as that of their male counterparts."[5]

During the course of World War II, women took on essential support roles in the UPA, which fought against the Soviet Union's occupation of territory formerly held by Nazi Germany from 1944 until 1949. Olena Petrenko notes that while women in the UPA primarily provided medical support, they also acted as ancillary fighters, messengers, and intelligence operatives.[6] Little is known about specific female fighters from this period, but as Marta Havryshko observes, "Thousands of women joined armed nationalist underground movements during and after [World War II] motivated by love, hate, patriotism, fear, and/or opportunity. Women served as nurses, messengers, couriers, secretaries, bodyguards, scouts and soldiers. Some of them became military instructors, junior officers, spies, investigators and even [underground intelligence] leaders of the lower ranks."[7]

By and large, women in the Ukrainian nationalist underground were treated the same as their male counterparts: they were subject to arrest, imprisonment, torture, sexual violence, and extrajudicial killing by the Nazi Gestapo, the Soviet Red Army, the Soviet secret police, and the Polish Communist authorities. Some were even successfully turned and became Soviet agents.[8] But women were allowed more personal freedom within the UPA than they would otherwise have had in society in general at that time. This freedom made women in the UPA effective members of an insurgency. Women "functioned as the support system of an insurgency that was dependent on the local population. It was the ties of the UPA women that made these connections happen: they were the ones who had established links to the towns and, in many places, they were trusted more so than the males. They were a far more visible target to state oppression than their male partners because of their location and roles."[9] In addition to the practical functions they fulfilled, the involvement of Ukrainian women in World War II had symbolic value as a sign of the whole nation's commitment to an independent Ukrainian state.

The history of these early Ukrainian nationalist organizations is central to today's conflict. First, the strain of nationalism they espoused remains prominent. For example, Dmytro Yarosh, the leader of Pravy Sektor—a right-wing political party and paramilitary group—styles himself as a soldier of "the national revolution" and a modern-day Stepan Bandera. Bandera's branch of the OUN collaborated with the Nazis with the goal of achieving an independent Ukrainian state. Bandera's hopes were dashed in June 1941 following the Declaration of the Ukrainian State Act in Lviv, which the Gestapo used as a pretext for arresting many OUN leaders. Yet, decades later, echoes of Bandera's right-wing nationalism remain strong.

Yarosh argues that Pravy Sektor helps defend against Russian and Western influences and that its armed wing is necessary to protect Ukraine from "internal occupiers." Furthermore, despite what could be defined as an exclusivist ideology (one that banned the participation of Jews and Poles), World War II–era Ukrainian nationalist organizations included women. Women occupied different roles than men but were acknowledged members of these armed groups and performed important operational functions. This historical involvement laid the groundwork for women's participation in far-right nationalist militias in the current conflict.

Women's Contemporary Mobilization: From the Euromaidan to War

When political protests erupted in Kyiv in November 2013, women formed an integral part of the protests and were the public face of what is known as the Euromaidan movement, which began in opposition to the decision by then-president Viktor Yanukovych not to sign a European Union association agreement and instead seek closer ties to Russia. Women were prominently featured in popular magazines' depictions of the Euromaidan protests, and millions watched women advocate for their cause on YouTube videos.[10] However, the symbolic weight given to women's participation in the Euromaidan movement was not matched by their on-the-ground experiences.

Jennifer Mathers's analysis of the Euromaidan period stresses "the dichotomy that we so often see in wars between the masculinized front lines and the feminized home front."[11] Although between 41 and 47 percent of participants in the Euromaidan protests during the 2013–2014 period were female, Sarah Phillips's ethnography of the protests details how women's contributions to the movement were marginalized and their actions were limited to ones associated with the domestic sphere: cooking, cleaning, and administering services.[12] According to reports at the time, "At a table, women sliced cheese, sausages and pickled tomatoes for sandwiches. Some brewed hot tea, which they distributed to the men outside. Other women stood at a first aid station behind a table of pills and other medical supplies."[13] Olga Onuch and Tamara Martsenyuk's analysis finds that even among women actively involved in civil society groups, "female activists tended to (on average—not all) participate in the administrative tasks and were less frequent participants in direct action repertoires. Or, as one activist . . . put it, women were in charge of 'the two Ks, *Kukhnia* [kitchen] and *Kreativ* [creative, design, and public relations].'"[14]

As the protests grew increasingly violent, women's ability to participate in Euromaidan protests was circumscribed: "Women were physically banned from the [*sic*] participation in the 'dangerous' protest zones (for example, by establishing men's controlled roadblocks, by organizing bus trips to Euromaidan from other cities for men only, etc.). When the protests became violent, women were turned away from the barricades by men 'for their own protection.'"[15] The shift from political protest to armed conflict that accompanied the Russian invasion of Crimea on March 1, 2014, further diminished overall female participation. Women played a key role in providing supplies to family members who were effectively trapped on Ukrainian military bases in Crimea. Some went so far as to act as human shields, protecting Ukrainian troops during the invasion.[16] But instead of the generalized participation that was seen in the Euromaidan protests, women's roles were more clearly delineated. Women continued to serve as political spokespersons on both sides of the developing conflict, including as the acting foreign minister and the deputy minister of foreign affairs of the Donetsk People's Republic.[17] However, attention soon shifted away from the many female Euromaidan protestors toward a small number of high-profile female combatants.

Nadiya Savchenko stands as the exemplar of the female combatant phenomenon in Ukraine. The first female graduate of Ukraine's Air Force University, Savchenko was captured by pro-Russian forces while fighting in eastern Ukraine in June 2014. Subsequently smuggled across the border into Russia and imprisoned for murder, she was the focus of intense international media attention during her captivity. During her imprisonment she was elected to the Ukrainian parliament, the *Rada,* in absentia. Since her release in a May 2016 prisoner swap, Savchenko has remained active in Ukrainian politics and even floated a presidential campaign.[18] Although she is now an archetype, many more female fighters who have participated in the Ukraine conflict go unnamed.

Female Fighters in Ukrainian Armed Groups

To better understand the factors motivating female combatants in the Ukraine conflict, we analyzed a wide range of Russian, Ukrainian, and English online media sources, which include news reports from foreign press agencies such as Reuters, sources aimed at an international audience (e.g., the website of Euromaidan Press), and media directed at a regional Russian-speaking audience (e.g., Lenta.ru). We also extensively examined YouTube videos related to female combatants that were posted by organizations as diverse as Radio Free Europe, Vice News, and Antimaidan Ukraine (a pro-Russia outfit). The videos ranged in length from approximately ninety seconds to twelve minutes. Videos were selected first through the YouTube search engine and later through the "suggested videos" function. The videos vary in the amount of attention paid to women. Some are specifically focused on female combatants; others mention women within a broader narrative about the conflict. These sources are not a representative sample of the entire universe of media reports and propaganda related to the Ukraine conflict and women's experiences in the conflict. However, they are illustrative of the *range* of women's motivations in joining the conflict and, despite limitations, provide important insights into women's roles.

Women are fighting on all sides of this conflict, in both the Ukrainian military and in a variety of nonstate armed groups.[19] Though the exact numbers of women fighting for various groups are impossible to determine based on the available information, women are clearly present in the pro-Russia separatist forces in the Donbass. (Attempts to contact representatives of the Donetsk People's Republic and the Luhansk People's Republic went unanswered.) Women have risen to prominence in the right-wing Aidar and Azov battalions that support the Ukrainian government, as well as in other government-aligned militias. Women do play important roles as fighters but also have an outsize role in communications and propaganda. Whenever and wherever women are present in armed groups, the media is invited to speak with them. Nevertheless, men still make up the overwhelming majority of fighters in eastern Ukraine, and the existence of all-male units is commonplace.[20]

Ukrainian women participate in a range of activities, including combat training. Many videos feature women assembling and loading firearms and participating in basic training–styled exercises, including firing on shooting ranges.[21] One video shows female medics participating in battlefield training exercises.[22] At the same time, it is clear that women's roles vary situationally, and versatility of skill is prized. "She goes into the field to rescue our fighters when they are wounded . . . plus she is our best sniper . . . she can cook for us, she can drive our tank," noted one male rebel commander concerning one of his female fighters, a former kindergarten secretary from the eastern city of Shakhtarsk in the Donetsk region.[23]

When it comes to women's actual participation in armed combat, many of the available battlefield accounts are simply unverifiable.[24] Amandine Regamey has studied largely unsubstantiated rumors of female snipers on both sides of the conflict. She details how, in January 2015, multiple Ukrainian media organizations reported that a special operations unit of the Ukrainian Armed Forces (Zbroyni Syly Ukrayiny) in the Donbass had arrested a nineteen-year-old female sniper who allegedly operated under the nickname "Ekstazi" and had killed at least ten Ukrainian soldiers. However, the evidence for these claims came mostly from the young woman's social media accounts.[25] Regamey argues that claims of female snipers in Ukraine arise from a conflation of the terms for "shooter" and "sniper" and are based on the historical trope of the skilled female sniper left over from the Second World War and Russia's war in Chechnya. At the same time, the legends propagated by both sides of the conflict are often rooted in reality. One female Chechen sniper in particular was described in Ukrainian television reports as a fighter with the Kyiv-2 battalion.[26] Thus, our analysis confirms that women are taking on a range of roles in armed groups in Ukraine, serving as medics, in logistics, on patrol, and as checkpoint guards, and most likely in combat as well.

While the specifics of women's day-to-day participation in warfighting are hard to come by, many of the reports provide a high level of detail about women's motivations. For example, a Russia Today video from June 2014 titled "Women's Battalions: Residents of Ukraine Stand Up for Their Cities" highlights multiple examples of female combatants.[27] The roughly four-minute video starts by introducing a young woman named Katerina. The narrator notes that the twenty-one-year old is fond of painting and can assemble a Kalashnikov automatic rifle in seconds. The scene then switches to a checkpoint near Luhansk, where another woman, Olesya, is in charge. She explains that taking up a machine gun is a matter of self-defense: "When your country is being threatened by fascists, there is no discussion."[28] "These are not the only women joining the combat forces," says the narrator, while the images change to show other video clips of female combatants from both sides of the conflict. The video includes a message from Anna Kovalenko, the leader of the pro-government 39th Women's Maidan Self-Defense Company (commonly known as the 39th Women's Company), calling for women to join the fight. Similarly, a ten-plus-minute video posted in June 2015 by Antimaidan Ukraine on the website of Abkhazian Network News Agency (ANNA) features eight women fighting in eastern Ukraine.[29] The video starts by introducing them by name and call sign. Most of the women are Ukrainians, with one foreign Russian volunteer. Throughout the video the women relay their different reasons for joining the fighting and share their understanding of the conflict and the effect it has had on their lives. The video ends with footage of women training at a shooting range.

At the individual level, the motivations of women participating in the conflict vary significantly within the two categories of nonstate armed groups: pro-government and separatist. Women in government-aligned forces are strongly motivated by Ukrainian nationalism. Women in the rebel groups, while sometimes identifying with the separatist cause, are more likely to list personal motivations, like protection of family or home. Those supporting the central government are more "offensive" in their orientation, actively choosing to go to the front. Those on the separatist side feel as if the front came to them.

Women in Pro-Government Armed Groups

From the outset of the armed conflict in eastern Ukraine, the Ukrainian Armed Forces were supplemented by roughly thirty volunteer battalions that were self-funded—often by a single wealthy patron. Many of these battalions have since been formally incorporated into the military. Women are active in these militias, some of which are affiliated with Pravy Sektor, though the majority of combatants are men.[30]

The most prominent of the pro-government battalions with female fighters is the 39th Women's Company.[31] Emerging from the self-defense units organized during the Euromaidan protests, the 39th Women's Company formed in mid-January 2014 specifically to counter separatists in the southern and eastern regions of Ukraine. Members promote themselves as pioneers of civil society in Ukraine, and the group is widely visible in social media. Their leader, Anna Kovalenko, was an adviser to several Ukrainian ministers of defense and once held a Woodrow Wilson Center fellowship in recognition of her role as a civil society leader. She has actively campaigned for more women to be involved in combat forces, arguing that "by protecting their country they are doing the right thing."[32]

Women in Ukrainian nationalist militias tend to be younger in age than their counterparts in separatist groups; typically they are in their late teens or early twenties. This is a generation of single young women who grew up in—and strongly identifies with—an independent, post-Soviet Ukraine. Generally they feel an obligation to support the Ukrainian state due to a sense of Ukrainian nationalism. Hailing from western regions of the country, such as Ivano-Frankivsk, Kyiv, and Vinnytsia, the women fighting on the pro-government side of the conflict rarely have personal ties to eastern Ukraine and are often stationed in areas far from their families, which possibly gives them a greater sense of independence. Rather than feeling as though they have been forced into fighting, these women actively sought out roles in the militias. Their proactive, "offensive" orientation is one key trait that distinguishes women in nationalist militias from their counterparts in separatist rebel groups.

There also appear to be additional motivations for women to join nationalist armed groups beyond this shared sense of Ukrainian nationalism. Some women in nationalist militias seem to view their participation as an avenue for gaining male attention or they join for other personal reasons. In recounting her journey to the front lines of the conflict, one volunteer in the pro-Ukrainian government Aidar battalion reflected on her resentment at being held back from the front by her boyfriend: "That bastard went to the front without me. He went to work and told me to wait for him in Kyiv. I did for some time. Then he disappeared for two months and I found out he had volunteered to go to the front."[33] She relates her feeling of betrayal that her boyfriend did not consider her capable of fighting with him against the rebels in the east. She eventually followed him to the front and, when he asked her to return home, she ignored his request and joined the Aidar battalion as a fighter.

Other women appear to glorify their newfound ability to engage in violence. Vita Zaverukha stands out in this respect. The teenager became notorious in the Russian press for her calls to wipe out all of Ukraine's Russian-speaking population and for posting neo-Nazi propaganda on her page on VKontakte (the Russian equivalent of Facebook).[34] Originally from Vinnytsia, Zaverukha joined the right-wing Aidar battalion as a seventeen-year-old and regularly posted social media photos of herself with other soldiers and weaponry. In November 2014 the magazine *Elle France* profiled Zaverukha as part of an interview conducted with pro-government female fighters in Luhansk. The article ran with the headline "They Were Students, Secretaries or Fashion Journalists: From the Maidan Revolution to the War against the Russian Separatists, Ukrainian Women Are Now on All the Fronts." Eventually the release of the article led to an apology by the magazine's editorial board for its failure to acknowledge her neo-Nazi background.[35] It is unclear exactly when Zaverukha ended her participation in the conflict; she was arrested in May 2015 for her role in an armed robbery in Kyiv that resulted in the deaths of two police officers. After she was released on bail in January 2017, Zaverukha and her partner were attacked by fellow members of an ultranationalist group to which they belonged.[36] In July 2017 both Zaverukha and her partner allegedly led an attack on transgender activists in Kyiv.[37] This descent from being hailed as the "Joan of Arc" of the Ukraine conflict to general criminality suggests that women's pathways into and out of nonstate armed groups are anything but straightforward.

Another prominent woman in Ukrainian ultranationalist armed groups was Anastasia Gorbacheva. Originally from Chernivtsi, Gorbacheva drew on her prior experience as a nurse while serving as a combat medic in a battalion affiliated with Pravy Sektor. Although within the ranks Gorbacheva was regarded as a good shooter, she was more widely known for her role as a Pravy Sektor spokesperson. She argued that the group would reject the result of any peace negotiations that it had not participated in.[38] In August 2015 she was killed at the age of thirty-two in an apartment in Mariupol by a gunshot to the chest.[39] It was unclear at the time whether Gorbacheva's death should be classified as murder or suicide; she was in a relationship with another fighter and several months pregnant.[40]

Women in Separatist Armed Groups

The groups fighting for autonomy or independence in eastern Ukraine primarily draw on support from their home regions—Donetsk and Luhansk—in addition to so-called foreign volunteers from Russia. Separatists first declared independent republic status in these two Ukrainian provinces in April 2014, and by the summer of that year popular support for the republics amounted to approximately one-third of the local populations. Research suggests that local support for armed separatist groups was driven by multiple factors: the potential negative economic effects for these regions as a result of joining the European Union, the Ukrainian government's embrace of the nationalist far-right, and perceived violations of the post-Soviet social contract, including Kyiv's attempt to annul a law supporting the use of the Russian language.[41] Multiple media interviews with members of these groups feature female commanders, artillery soldiers, and snipers, showing them in an array of combat-related roles.[42]

Women in the Donbass rebel groups tend to be older than their pro-Ukrainian counterparts; many are mothers and wives. In one interview, Yelena Dustova, a thirty-nine-year-old mother of three, argues, "What, should I allow them to shoot at me in my town? No. I will stand here so that they won't be allowed to pass. I have my mom and my kids in there."[43] In these groups women often present a "defensive" narrative that is focused on the need to protect from potential loss what they already possess: their families, their homes, and their land.[44] They perceive the pro-Ukrainian side as the aggressor. In a moment of reflection Ilona Banevich, a separatist militia commander, observes: "I don't know if it's heroism or not. The people are just fighting for their homeland. We didn't go to them; they themselves came to us, claiming to protect us."[45] Another older woman observes that there is nothing unnatural about taking up arms—even for an ordinary civilian woman who happens to be an excellent cook—if one is surrounded by war and finds her land is threatened.[46] One younger female rebel group commander, whose stated goal is to destroy the right-wing government-aligned battalions, refers to a different sense of abandonment: of being left behind to fend for oneself.[47] Her narrative is one in which shameless men have left behind "fragile girls" to protect their homes and their lands. In this view, women's participation in armed conflict is exceptional and the result of men's failures. While this narrative is likely crafted in part to goad men into joining the rebel groups, it does differentiate the motives of the separatist groups from those held by the pro-government ones.

The willingness of these women to fight defensively is in line with findings from other conflicts: when viewing war as a struggle for legitimate defense of home and community, women tend to be just as much in favor of war as men are.[48] The sense of a perceived obligation to fight conveyed by many women in the separatist groups is well illustrated by a four-minute staged address posted by Vox Populi Evo.[49] It starts with footage of a self-propelled artillery unit firing a series of shots. The video then switches to a picture of five women standing in a row, facing the camera. The women in the video are of different ages and arguably represent the children, wives, and mothers of the men fighting on the rebels' side. The first woman approaches the camera and addresses the pro-Ukrainian forces: "Soldiers, officers of the Ukrainian Army! Every day the war, started by the government of Ukraine against the people of the Donbass, brings grief. Not only to our families, but to yours." The women then take turns delivering their speeches. They emphasize that despite the devastating consequences of the conflict, they do not hold malice against pro-government soldiers: "We understand that every killed soldier is a grief for your families. And when our husbands have to shoot at you, protecting our children, we understand that it is a huge tragedy." Each one speaks about the devastation and fear brought by war to both sides of the conflict. They argue that official Ukrainian propaganda misleads soldiers, distorting reality and sending them to fratricidal war: "Guys! You were just betrayed and left to die for the interests of American politicians and oligarchs . . . oligarchs and neo-Nazis will betray you again, just like they did many times before." The women call on Ukrainian soldiers to stop destroying their homeland and recognize the independence of the Donbass: "Our sons, brothers, husbands, and us, women, took weapons! We love our motherland and will protect its freedom and independence with weapons in our hands. And, if needed, we are ready to sacrifice our lives for our home and a peaceful sky above our children!"

Many sources also stress the necessity of female participation on the separatist side as a result of manpower shortages. For example, in a May 2014 video Igor Strelkov—a prominent separatist leader in Donetsk— claimed that, "Donetsk needs defenders, separatists who are volunteer soldiers, who are disciplined. If men are not capable of this, we will have to call on women."[50] He continued to lament the absence of female officers in the Ukrainian military and reserves, whom he could call on to defect to the rebel side. But he also asked, "What difference does it make when no officers are coming to us at all?" In early 2015 the Ukrainian military announced its own mobilization of women between the ages of twenty and fifty, due to manpower shortages.[51] When Katerina, a twenty-one-year-old medic who first joined the front lines as a nurse, was asked by an interviewer whether she had to kill, she replied, "Yes, it was necessary for protection. That is, they came to us, not us to them."[52] Ultimately it is unclear the degree to which a manpower shortage factors into women's recruitment and prominence within separatist armed groups. While relevant, such shortages do not seem like a sufficient explanation for women's extensive engagement with the conflict.

The question of a manpower shortage has also been linked to the prominence of Russian volunteers, or "little green men"—suspected regular Russian military officers fighting on behalf of the rebels—in the conflict in Ukraine. However, there appear to be relatively few "little green women." In several videos female volunteers identify themselves as Russian nationals, and one report names a Belarusian.[53] Other reports allege that many Russian-born women are fighting for the separatists but with scant evidence to support the claim. While some Russian-born women may be involved in the conflict on the side of the separatist armed groups, their participation is not so extensive as to influence the conflict in any significant way.

Conclusions

While men make up the vast majority of fighters in Ukraine, women constitute a recognizable minority. Our analysis of female participation in Ukraine shows that female combatants should not be viewed as the single category of "women." Significant variation in women's roles and motivations exists across the different armed groups as well as within specific armed groups. Our main findings are as follows:

- Important demographic differences exist across nonstate armed groups operating in Ukraine. Women in nationalist groups tend to be younger, unmarried, and from western regions, while women in separatist groups are older, have familial responsibilities, and operate in their home regions of Donetsk and Luhansk.
- Women take on both combat and typical noncombat roles within both types of groups. While women appear to be universally trained to bear arms, they also play important support and logistical roles.
- A manpower shortage is likely driving some female participation in the conflict, particularly among the Donbass groups, but nationalist ideology is also a motivating factor that needs to be taken seriously.
- Demobilization and other post-conflict programs should be responsive to the conditions that motivate women to participate. In the case of Ukraine, this motivation varies significantly across armed groups.

Many civil wars are rooted in competing nationalisms similar to the ones fueling the war in Ukraine. Although some scholars suggest that nationalism may work against women's participation in conflict by reinforcing gender hierarchies, a recent analysis of the prevalence of female combatants within rebel groups does not support this theory.[54] Nationalist conflicts, like the civil wars in Sri Lanka and Northern Ireland, for example, often mobilize female fighters.[55] In these contexts women's participation can be quite fluid; women can take up combat positions and then return to support roles based on operational needs. This pattern is reflected in women's roles in the current conflict in Ukraine.

The differences in the motivations behind female participation among separatist and nationalist armed groups in Ukraine derive from both the ideologies of the groups and their positions in the conflict. Even though each side is pursuing its own nationalist agenda, perceptions regarding which side is the aggressor and which is the victim are important. Fighters on the Ukrainian government side present a narrative of choice; fighters on the rebel side argue that participation in the conflict is not optional but rather is a necessary defensive step. A July 2014 Russia Today segment that profiles women on both sides of the conflict captures these competing narratives of self-defense and ultra-nationalism.[56] Differences in the ages and family status of female combatants also contribute to diverging rationales for participation. Manpower shortages, when mentioned, are typically related to the unwillingness of men to fight for the separatist groups and women's need to compensate for this.

While we can draw some conclusions about why women are fighting on behalf of separatist groups in Donetsk and Luhansk, their motivations may be evolving over time and may inform only some of the roles that women hold within these organizations. Indeed, research on women's participation in the World War II–era UPA suggests that there are always exceptions to the general patterns described here. While single, childless women predominantly joined the UPA, some mothers did as well. Some women joined because of romantic connections to men in the group, but others did not possess this motivation.[57] This suggests that individual-level motivations for joining armed groups should be followed closely as a conflict continues.

Despite the fact that both Ukrainian state leaders and the leaders of various armed factions called on women to join the conflict, many of the women participating in political violence in Ukraine continue to have a relatively unequal status within the nonstate armed groups. As Miranda Alison notes, active and ongoing conflict leaves less time for reflections on gender and female emancipation.[58] While the space for female participation is greater within irregular, nonstate armed groups compared to the more formally rigid and hierarchical structure of the Ukrainian military, women are participating in groups (specifically right-wing militias) that traditionally would be hostile to the emancipation of women. Further research on violent extremism and the reasons why women are drawn to exclusivist groups will help shed some light on this phenomenon.

The degree to which nationalist ideology is entrenched in this conflict suggests that any outright victory by one side (and its attendant version of nationalism) will further fracture Ukrainian society. Women in the separatist groups do not necessarily believe they are fighting *against* the Ukrainian state. Rather, many argue that they are fighting to protect their families and communities as a self-defense force. But this narrative is rejected by those supporting the Ukrainian government. In a post-conflict environment, the contributions of women fighting on the rebel side likely will be overlooked at both the local and national levels. This will put former insurgent women in a vulnerable position once the conflict ends. This dynamic can be seen in other cases, such as the war for Eritrean independence, in which women who fought were largely excluded from changes in the postwar social order.[59] Any peaceful resolution to the conflict will have to take into account the wide variation in the roles women play on the two sides (combat, support, communications, etc.) and be responsive to the many factors motivating women's participation.

Notes

Epigraph: Novosti 2015. Opolchenka s poz'vnim "Belka" (News 2015, Militia member with the call sign "Squirrel"), YouTube video, 1:49, posted by Novosti 2015, June 18, 2015, https://www.youtube.com/watch?v=AQF4iN97lco.

1. Laura Sjoberg, "Jihadi Brides and Female Volunteers: Reading the Islamic State's War to See Gender and Agency in Conflict Dynamics," *Conflict Management and Peace Science* 35, no. 3 (2017): 296–311, doi:10.1177/0738894217695050.

2. *Na Donbasse mir i voina v zhenskikh rukakh* (In Donbass peace and war are in the hands of women), YouTube video, 10:28, posted by ANNA News, May 7, 2015, https://www.youtube.com/watch?v=FXT3IvtSlm8.

3. Alan Taylor, "Beauty in the Ceasefire: A Pageant in Donetsk," *Atlantic*, March 9, 2015, https://www.theatlantic.com/photo/2015/03/beauty-in-the-ceasefire-a-pageant-in-donetsk/387247/.

4. Larysa Zariczniak, "Violence and the UPA Women: Experiences and Influences," *European Historical Studies Electronic Journal* 94, no. 2 (2015): 245, http://eustudies.history.knu.ua/larisa-zarichnyak-violence-and-the-upa-woman-experiences-and-influences/.

5. Zariczniak, "Violence and the UPA Women," 243–44.

6. Olena Petrenko, "Anatomy of the Unsaid: Along the Taboo Lines of Female Participation in the Ukrainian Nationalistic Underground," in *Women and Men at War: A Gender Perspective on World War II and Its Aftermath in Central and Eastern Europe*, ed. Maren Röger and Ruth Leiserowitz (Osnabrück, Germany: Fibre Verlag, 2012), 251.

7. Marta Havryshko, "Illegitimate Sexual Practices in the OUN Underground and the UPA in Western Ukraine in the 1940s and 1950s," *Journal of Power Institutions in Post-Soviet Societies* 17 (2016): 6, doi:10670/1.zykqn7.

8. Jeffrey Burds, "Gender and Policing in Soviet West Ukraine, 1944–1948," *Cahiers du Monde Russe* 42, nos. 2–4 (2001): 279–320, doi:10.4000/monderusse.8454.

9. Zariczniak, "Violence and the UPA Women," 19.

10. Rebecca Moss, "Women Stand at the Frontlines of the Euromaidan Protest in Kiev," *Elle*, February 21, 2014, http://www.elle.com/culture/career-politics/news /a24362/womens-opposition-euromaidan-protest-kiev/.

11. Jennifer G. Mathers, "Gender, Heroism, and Women in the Ukraine Crisis," paper presented at the European Consortium for Political Research Conference, Uppsala, Sweden, June 12, 2015, 3, https://ecpr.eu/Events/PaperDetails .aspx?PaperID=23102&EventID=100.

12. Sarah D. Phillips, "The Women's Squad in Ukraine's Protests: Feminism, Nationalism, and Militarism on the Maidan," *American Ethnologist* 41, no. 3 (2014): 414–26, doi:10.1111/amet.12093; Iryna Stelmakh and Tom Balmforth, "Ukraine's Maidan Protests—One Year On," *Guardian*, November 21, 2014, http://www.the guardian.com/world/2014/nov/21/-sp-ukraine-maidan-protest-kiev.

13. Ari Shapiro, "Molotov Cocktails and Razor Wire: Inside an Occupied Building in Ukraine," NPR, April 11, 2014, https://www.npr.org/sections/thetwo -way/2014/04/11/301759073/molotov-cocktails-and-razor-wire-inside-an -occupied-building-in-ukraine.

14. Olga Onuch and Tamara Martsenyuk, "Mothers and Daughters of the Maidan: Gender, Repertoires of Violence, and the Division of Labour in Ukrainian Protests," *Social, Health, and Communication Studies Journal* 1, no. 1 (2014): 115, https://journals.macewan.ca/shcsjournal/article/view/248.

15. Onuch and Martsenyuk, "Mothers and Daughters of the Maidan," 118.

16. Mathers, "Gender, Heroism, and Women," 10.

17. Griff Witte and William Booth, "As Russian Forces Escalate, Ukraine's Influence Waning," *Washington Post*, April 26, 2014, https://www.washington post.com/world/europe/as-russian-forces-escalate-ukraines-influence -waning/2014/04/25/efb5a306-048f-4599-aabe-97e3d6005e54_story.html; D. Garrison Golubock, "Both Sides in Ukraine Standoff Call for New Tactics," *Moscow Times,* May 18, 2014, https://themoscowtimes.com/articles/both-sides -in-ukraine-standoff-call-for-new-tactics-35537; "Ministry Structure," Ministry of Foreign Affairs of the Donetsk People's Republic, accessed August 28, 2018, http://mid-dnr.ru/en/pages/ministry-structure/.

18. Alec Luhn, "Nadiya Savchenko: 'Ukraine, If You Need Me to Be President, I Will,'" *Guardian*, May 27, 2016, https://www.theguardian.com/world/2016/may /27/nadiya-savchenko-ukraine-if-you-need-me-to-be-president-i-will.

19. Rick Lyman, "Ukraine Rebels Upbeat after an Infusion of Aid," *New York Times*, February 2, 2015, http://www.nytimes.com/2015/02/03/world/europe/on -front-lines-in-ukraine-rebels-are-upbeat-and-eager-to-advance.html.

20. Kenneth Dickerman, "Inside a Volunteer Paramilitary Unit on the Front Lines in Ukraine," *Washington Post*, May 3, 2016, http://www.washingtonpost

.com/news/in-sight/wp/2016/05/03/inside-a-volunteer-paramilitary-unit-on-the
-front-lines-in-ukraine.

21. *Zhinky hotuyut'sya do sluzhby u Zbrojnyx Sylax Ukrayiny* (Women pre-
pare for service in the armed forces of Ukraine), YouTube video, 2:41, posted by
Mistotvpoltava, March 30, 2015, https://www.youtube.com/watch?v=GDRZQ
qghHQrk; *Donbass Women Fight against Ukraine's Invasion for Their Children and
Motherland*, YouTube video, 10:28, posted by Antimaidan Ukraine, June 26, 2015,
http://www.youtube.com/watch?v=9sfz_OfWQ8s.

22. *Zhinky v pohonax vchylysya ryatuvaty soldat* (Women in uniform were
learning to rescue soldiers), YouTube video, 1:54, posted by Telekompaniya
M-Studio, November 29, 2014, https://www.youtube.com/watch?v=7-uki8iFXns.

23. Lyman, "Ukraine Rebels Upbeat."

24. *Interviu—26-letniaia sibiriachka v Donbasse* (Interview—twenty-six-year
-old Siberian girl in the Donbass), YouTube video, 2:32, posted by Novosti. Sobytiia.
Fakty, October 5, 2014, http://www.youtube.com/watch?v=KBUjCCLQtSk?.

25. Amandine Regamey, "Falsehood in the War in Ukraine: The Legend of
Women Snipers," *Journal of Power Institutions in Post-Soviet Societies* 17 (2016):
3, doi:10670/1.git6x4.

26. *Zhinky-vijs'kovi u zoni ATO voyuyut' na rivni z cholovikamy* (Military
women in the ATO zone are at war with men), YouTube video, 8:37, posted by
TCH, November 9, 2014, https://www.youtube.com/watch?v=kY6SO4OnZ2o.

27. *Zhenskie batalony: zhitelnitsy Ukrainy vstaiut na zashchitu svoikh gorodov*
(Female battalions: Ukrainian women stand up to protect their cities), YouTube
video, 3:39, posted by Russia Today, July 2, 2014, http://www.youtube.com/watch
?v=GNf4uzNXuQo.

28. *Zhenskie batalony.*

29. *Donbass Women Fight against Ukraine's Invasion.*

30. "Commander of Ukraine's army Nayev invites volunteer fighters to join
regular troops," UNIAN, July 25, 2018, https://www.unian.info/society/10200258
-commander-of-ukraine-s-army-nayev-invites-volunteer-fighters-to-join-regular
-troops.html.

31. *Zhinocha sotnya No. 39, abo zhinky v umovax vijny* (39th Women's Company, or women in wartime), YouTube video, 21:06, posted by Zhinocha sotnia # 39
samooborony, June 14, 2014, http://www.youtube.com/watch?v=pInh_rQN9Wo.

32. *Zhenskie batalony.*

33. Elena Savchuk, "The Women Fighting on the Frontline in Ukraine,"
Guardian, March 5, 2015, https://www.theguardian.com/world/2015/mar/05
/ukraine-women-fighting-frontline.

34. Marina Tishchenko, "Po podozreniiu v rasstrele militsionerov zaderzhana
19-letniaia Vita Zaverukha" (Nineteen-year-old Vita Zaverukha is arrested on
suspicion of shooting police officers), *Komsomolskaya Pravda v Ukraine,* May 6,

2016, http://kp.ua/incidents/499896-po-podozrenyui-v-rasstrele-mylytsyonerov
-zaderzh ana-19-letniaia-vyta-zaverukha.

35. Will Stewart, "Teenage Girl Soldier Hailed as Ukraine's 'Joan of Arc' Is
Revealed as Neo-Nazi and Is Arrested over Cop Killing," *Daily Mail Online*, May 8,
2015, http://www.dailymail.co.uk/news/article-3073478/Teen-girl-feted-Ukraine-s
-Joan-Arc-fighting-against-Russian-rebels-revealed-nasty-neo-Nazi-views-arrested
-killing-cops.html.

36. Tat'yana Nechet, "Muzh Zaverukhi zayavil, chto ih izbili byvshie
pobratimy" (Zaverukha's husband says they were beaten by their C-14 brothers),
Komsomolskaya Pravda v Ukraine, February 13, 2017, https://kp.ua/incidents
/566827-muzh-zaverukhy-zaiavyl-chto-ykh-yzbyly-byvshye-pobratymy.

37. Aleksei Reutin, "V ozhidanii suda: Neonacistka Vita Zaveruha poluchila
ugrozy ot MVD Ukrainy" (Waiting for trial: Neo-Nazi Vita Zaverukha receives
threats from the Ministry of Internal Affairs of Ukraine), and *PolitEkspert*, March
3, 2017, https://politexpert.net/31448-v-ozhidanii-suda-neonacistka-vita-zaveruha
-poluchila-ugrozy-ot-mvd-ukrainy.

38. "Razvedchista 'Pravogo Sektora' porazila zritelei ukrainskogo TV bessvy-
aznoi rech'iu," (Pravy Sektor intelligence officer amazed Ukrainian TV watchers
with an incoherent speech), TV Zvezda video, 0:56, March 11, 2015, https://tvz
vezda.ru/news/vstrane_i_mire/content/201503110830-s4qq.htm.

39. "Stalo izvestno, kak pogibla razvedchitsa 'Pravoro sektora'" (It is known
how the intelligence officer of "Pravy sektor" died), TV Zvezda video, 0:50,
August 10, 2015, https://tvzvezda.ru/news/vstrane_i_mire/content/201508101614
-6ran.htm.

40. Alena Katashinskaya, "V zone ATO pogibla razvedchitsa 'Pravoro sek-
topa' c pozyvnym 'Lisa,'" ("Pravy sector" intelligence officer, code named "Fox,"
died in the ATO zone), *Komsomolskaya Pravda v Ukraine*, August 9, 2015, https://
kp.ua/incidents/508546-v-zone-ato-pohybla-razvedchytsa-pravoho-sektora-s
-pozyvnym-lysa.

41. Elise Guiliano, "The Origins of Separatism: Popular Grievances in Donetsk
and Luhansk," *PONARS Eurasia*, October 2015, http://www.ponarseurasia.org
/memo/origins-separatism-popular-grievances-donetsk-and-luhansk.

42. *Interviu s komandirom gaybichnoj batarei 'Gajkoj'* (Interview with the
commander of the howitzer battery, "Gadget"), YouTube video, 2:23, posted by
Andrei Stalinov, January 23, 2015, https://www.youtube.com/watch?v=Wrl
KZifNdZU.

43. John Wendle, "Ukraine Women's Battalion Mans Barricades," Al Jazeera,
June 3, 2014, http://www.aljazeera.com/indepth/features/2014/06/ukraine-women
-battalion-mans-barricades-201463132521484197.html.

44. *Address of Donbass Women to Armed Forces of Ukraine*, YouTube video,
3:45, posted by Vox Populi Evo, August 13, 2015, http://www.youtube.com

/watch?v=CetyWFCUkl4; *Zhenskie batalony*; *Zapretnii Donbass. Snaiper 'Ptitsa'.*
Zhenshini v opolchenii (Forbidden Donbass. Sniper "Bird." Women in militias),
YouTube video, 3:11, posted by 17 News, February 23, 2015, https://www.youtube
.com/watch?v=T5cZ2yiZIzM.

45. *Ilona Banevich–komandir otriada opolchentsev* (Ilona Banevich-
commander of the militia squad), YouTube video, 4:00, posted by Dom Faktov,
March 26, 2015, http://www.youtube.com/watch?v=icM3fw7KVh8. Account
deactivated by YouTube.

46. *Zhenskie batalony.*

47. *Novosti 2015.*

48. *Miranda Alison*, Women and Political Violence: Female Combatants in
Ethno-National Conflict (New York: Routledge, 2009), 113.

49. *Address of Donbass Women to Armed Forces of Ukraine.*

50. Golubock, "Both Sides in Ukraine Standoff."

51. "U Genshtabi zaiavyly, shcho 'pri neobkhidnosti' mozhut mobilizuvaty
zhinok vid 20 rokiv" (The general staff said that "if necessary" it is possible to
mobilize women as young as twenty years old), UNIAN, February 4, 2015, http://
www.unian.ua/politics/1040064-u-genshtabi-zayavili-scho-pri-neobhidnosti
-mojut-mobilizuvati-jinok-vid-20-rokiv.html.

52. *Zhenskie batalony.*

53. *Interviu—26-letniaia sibiriachka v Donbasse*; *Na Donbasse mir i voina v
zhenskikh rukakh*; "Zhenshini 'Novorossii': voina na Ukraine kak start kar'eri"
(Women of "Novorussia": war in Ukraine as a career start), BBC, October 13, 2017,
http://www.bbc.com/russian/international/2014/10/141013_tr_novorussia_
women; Ol'ga Omel'yanchuk, "Terroristy v yubkakh: za "LNR" i "DNR" voyuyut
sotni zhenshin" (Terrorists in skirts: hundreds of women are fighting for the LNR
and DNR), *Obozrevatel*, November 16, 2015, https://www.obozrevatel.com/crime
/48632-terroristyi-v-yubkah-ubivayut-bez-zhalosti-i-sluzhat-v-rossijskoj-armii
.htm.

54. Mary Caprioli, "Primed for Violence: The Role of Gender Inequality in
Predicting Internal Conflict," *International Studies Quarterly* 49, no. 9 (2005):
161–78, doi:10.1111/j.0020-8833.2005.00340.x; Jakana L. Thomas and Reed M.
Wood, "The Social Origins of Female Combatants," *Conflict Management and
Peace Science* (2017): 1–18, doi:10.1177/0738894217695524.

55. Alison, *Women and Political Violence*; Miranda Alison, "Cogs in the
Wheel? Women in the Liberation Tigers of Tamil Eelam," *Civil Wars* 6, no. 4
(2003): 37–54, doi:10.1080/1369824042000221367; Swati Parashar, "Feminist
International Relations and Women Militants: Case Studies from Sri Lanka and
Kashmir," *Cambridge Review of International Affairs* 22, no. 2 (2009): 235–56,
doi:10.1080/09557570902877968; Kim Jordan and Myriam Denov, "Birds of Freedom? Perspectives on Female Emancipation and Sri Lanka's Liberation Tigers of

Tamil Eelam," *Journal of International Women's Studies* 9, no. 1 (2007): 42–62, http://vc.bridgew.edu/jiws/vol9/iss1/3/.

56. *Zhenskie batalony.*

57. Zariczniak, "Violence and the UPA Women," 3.

58. Alison, *Women and Political Violence,* 117.

59. See, for example, Victoria Bernal, "Equality to Die For? Women Guerrilla Fighters and Eritrea's Cultural Revolution," *Political and Legal Anthropology Review* 23, no. 2 (2000): 61–76, doi:10.1525/pol.2000.23.2.61; and Sondra Hale, "Liberated, but Not Free: Women in Post-War Eritrea," in *The Aftermath: Women in Post-Conflict Transformation,* ed. Sheila Meintjes, Anu Pillay, and Meredeth Turshen (London: Zed, 2002).

2

The Kurdish Regions

Fighting as Kurds, Fighting as Women

Our society used to look at women only as "good housewives." Women were just made ready for men and locked up at home like a slave. But now we understand our bitter reality. We have changed now. We live, learn, and fight. We are soldiers now.

—JANDA, YPJ CAPTAIN

The onset of the Syrian Civil War has brought a range of new actors to prominence in the Middle East. One of the most important is the group calling itself the Islamic State (also known as ISIS). Another is the Kurdish PYD (or Democratic Union Party), whose armed forces have gained prominence not only for their military effectiveness against ISIS (a characteristic that sharply distinguishes them from both the Syrian military and the main opposition groups) but also for the large number of female soldiers in their ranks. Given the explicit and violent misogyny espoused by ISIS, its frequent defeats at the hands of a fighting force that is, by most estimates, about 40 percent female, have been greeted with a substantial degree of schadenfreude by the international media. This high rate of participation by women is mirrored in the Kurdish national movement in Turkey. And yet it is far less true of the Kurdish armed movements in Iraq. Indeed, there are significant differences in women's participation in Kurdish nationalist politics across the political spectrum and in different parts of an area that, regardless of current internationally recognized borders, Kurds often refer to as "Kurdistan." In this chapter we compare the involvement of women in the armed wings of the major Kurdish armed movements in Turkey, Syria, and Iraq.

The Kurdish people number as many as thirty million, spread across Turkey, Syria, Iran, and Iraq. The historical experiences of Kurds in each of these states and their relationships with their respective regimes vary widely, as do the nature and intensity of political mobilization. The Turkish and Syrian Kurdish national movements (represented by the PKK, or the Kurdistan Workers Party, and the PYD, respectively) share the radical leftist ideology articulated by Abdullah Öcalan. By contrast, Iraqi Kurdish politics is dominated by the more conservative and personalist Kurdish Democratic Party (KDP) and the loosely leftist Patriotic Union of Kurdistan (PUK).

All of these political organizations have both political and armed wings. Some of the armed wings have separate names and others use the name of the political organization itself. The PKK's armed forces are usually referred to as "the PKK," while in Iraq the armed wings of the PUK and the KDP are collectively known as peshmerga (Kurdish for "those who face death"). In Syria the PYD has two associated armed wings: the YPG, the "People's Protection Units," and the YPJ, the "Women's Protection Units." The former

Figure 2.1 Map of Kurdish Regions

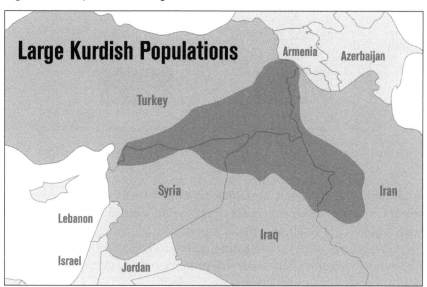

Figure 2.2 Kurdish Armed Groups

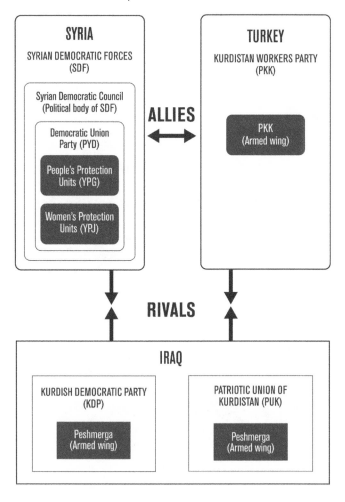

is all male and the latter all female, but the two forces train and fight together. Further confusing matters, the Syrian Kurdish forces have allied with a number of other non-Kurdish groups in northern Syria (including Sunni and Christian Arabs) to form the Syrian Democratic Forces (SDF)—an umbrella organization under US military patronage that has its own political body, the Syrian Democratic Council.

Women's positions within the Kurdish national movement—including their roles in the armed movements affiliated with the various organizations involved—are far from uniform. In fact, women's participation in Kurdish political life, particularly in armed conflict, varies a great deal from country to country. This variation, however, often goes unacknowledged in the Western media, which erases or elides the differences in women's participation in favor of the now-commonplace trope of the "badass Kurdish female guerrilla."[1] For instance, breathless coverage by *ABC News* of a group of women training to join the Zeravani, the military police unit of the Iraqi Kurdish forces, begins as follows: "The fighters that ISIS fears the most wear lipstick, according to these troops. Some even let their long braided hair fall out behind their hats."[2] The improbability of soldiers in the middle of a gun battle stopping to reapply their lipstick notwithstanding, this sort of coverage largely ignores the substantial differences among Kurdish armed groups with regard to their inclusion of female fighters. While the armed wings of the Syrian Kurdish forces (the YPG and the YPJ combined) and of the PKK are by many estimates about 40 percent female, the Iraqi Kurdish militias have a far smaller number of female fighters.[3]

Despite the fact that the Kurdish nationalist organizations in Syria, Turkey, and Iraq do share some features in common—all are, obviously, Kurdish nationalist, all are secular rather than religious, and all have been profoundly shaped by the individuals leading them—there are real differences among them. Differing ideologies and processes of Kurdish nationalist mobilization in each state have led to distinct modes of participation by Kurdish women in Turkey and Syria on the one hand, and in Iraq on the other. Comparisons between these organizations illuminate factors that facilitate or impede this mobilization and the impact of women's participation in, or exclusion from, nonstate armed groups on the organizations themselves. We begin with an overview of the Kurdish national movements in each state, followed by a discussion of the role women play in the armed wings of each movement, an analysis of the reasons for this variation, and the consequences both for the organizations in question and for geopolitics more broadly.

Kurdish Nationalism(s)

Despite the ethnic ties between Kurds in Syria, Turkey, and Iraq, the Kurdish political landscape varies widely by state. Although Kurds in all three countries have faced repression and attempts at state-sponsored cultural erasure, the groups' responses to these challenges have varied a great deal.

Turkey

Kurdish identity in Turkey is both politicized and contested by the Turkish state. Under the Ottoman Empire, a shared Sunni Muslim identity united the various ethnic minorities across the empire, including Kurds. But following the collapse of the empire after the First World War, Mustafa Kemal Ataturk undertook an ambitious state-building process. The goal of this process was the construction of a modern nation-state based on an ethnonational Turkish identity, a political project that could not accommodate a separate Kurdish ethnic identity. The early years of the Turkish Republic (established in 1923) were characterized by hostility between the central government in Ankara and the Kurdish regions. Kurdish attempts to establish autonomy (or, in some cases, independence) were met with violent repression by the Turkish state, including the Dersim Massacre of 1937. In the following decades the Turkish government passed laws intended to eradicate "Kurdishness" as a separate identity entirely, including enacting bans on teaching and speaking the Kurdish language.[4]

In the 1970s Turkey experienced a decade of political upheaval that culminated in the military coup of 1981, which precipitated a military crackdown on the Kurdish southeast. Tens of thousands of (mostly male) Kurds were arrested. It was in this context that the PKK was founded in 1978. Led by the charismatic ideologue Abdullah Öcalan, the PKK was Marxist in ideology and authoritarian in its internal organization. While the latter characteristic reflected a trend common across the global left, it took a particularly austere form within the PKK; one former member interviewed referred to it as "Stalinist."[5]

In 1984 the PKK launched an insurgency from its bases in Syria with the goal of establishing a separate Kurdish state. Throughout the 1980s and 1990s the PKK attacked both military and civilian targets, including police officers and other targets associated with the state, using both conventional tactics and, occasionally, terrorism, including suicide bombings. The PKK also targeted Kurdish "village guards," the local militias established by the Turkish state that Kurdish villagers had joined, often reluctantly. In the mid-1990s the Turkish military adopted a policy of eradicating villages considered support bases for the PKK, displacing between three hundred thousand and one million people from rural areas, mostly to the city of Diyarbakir.[6]

In 1999 the PKK suffered a major setback when Syria, seeking better relations with Turkey after the end of the Cold War, expelled Öcalan. Having lost his safe haven, Öcalan was soon arrested by Turkey. One immediate consequence was that the PKK's main training camps were relocated to Qandil, a mountainous region in Iraqi Kurdistan. Perhaps of equal consequence was that Öcalan's arrest led to an ideological evolution on the part of the PKK and its affiliates. Since the mid-2000s the PKK (and its Syrian ally, the PYD) have embraced a political model known as "democratic confederalism," which Öcalan came to espouse after reading the writings of American anarchist Murray Bookchin while in prison.[7] As a result, the PKK's objectives have shifted, from secession to autonomy within Turkey, local governance for the Kurdish regions, and greater respect for the rights of minorities more broadly.[8] But despite several attempts at a peace process (most recently from 2012 to 2015), the PKK's conflict with the Turkish state is ongoing.[9] The total number of casualties from the Kurdish insurgency in Turkey since 1978 is estimated at around forty thousand.[10]

Syria

The history of Syria's Kurdish community—constituting about 10 percent of Syria's total population before the onset of the Syrian Civil War but smaller than its counterparts in both Turkey and Iraq—is closely entwined with that of its larger neighbors. While Kurdish nationalism has existed in Syria since at least the end of the Ottoman period, divisions between urban and rural Kurdish elites prevented the emergence of a single Kurdish national movement throughout the first half of the twentieth century.[11] Kurds who became involved in politics often did so via the Syrian Communist Party until the late 1950s and early 1960s, when a more explicit Kurdish nationalism developed, driven in part by growing Kurdish resentment at their political and economic disenfranchisement. More robust Kurdish nationalist parties emerged, some with ties to those in Iraq.[12] Tensions with Damascus increased when the explicitly Arab nationalist Ba'ath Party rose to power in 1966. Kurdish towns received new Arabic names, and as in Turkey, teaching the Kurdish language was discouraged.[13] Kurdish activists faced arrest, torture, and even death at the hands of the secret police.[14]

Nevertheless, Hafez al Assad, who assumed the presidency in 1970, was more than willing to form an alliance with the PKK as a means of pressuring Turkey, despite his regime's hostility to Kurdish nationalism in Syria. The PKK established bases and training camps in northern Syria, and Kurdish Syrians were allowed to fight with the PKK as an alternative to Syrian military service. This had the additional benefit (for the Syrian state, at least) of directing nationalist activism among Syrian Kurds against the Turkish government rather than against the Syrian regime itself.

Assad's strategy ultimately proved to be a double-edged sword. After the relationship between the regime and the PKK soured, an independent Syrian Kurdish militant group (effectively a branch of the PKK) was established in 2003.[15] The new organization was named the PYD (Partiya Yekîtiya Demokrat, or Democratic Union Party), and it espoused the same broadly Marxist ideology as the PKK. Because of the PKK's history in Syria, when the PYD was founded it had a ready pool of recruits for its armed forces among Syrian Kurds who, with the Assad regime's encouragement, had received both military training and political indoctrination from the PKK.[16] Today the PYD still looks to Öcalan as its ideological leader, although its leadership is officially shared by two co-chairs, Shahoz Hasan and Aysha Hisso (both elected in September 2017). Former co-chair Salih Muslim also remains a significant figure in the party.[17]

The eruption of the Syrian Civil War and the encroachment of ISIS into Syria's Kurdish regions prompted the PYD to establish two new armed wings—the YPG and the YPJ. The deterioration of the Syrian state eventually led to the establishment of three autonomous Kurdish cantons in northern Syria collectively referred to as Rojava, all governed through the system of "direct democracy" espoused by Öcalan.[18]

Iraq

In contrast to the important role played by the PKK and Öcalan in Kurdish politics in both Syria and Turkey, political life in Iraqi Kurdistan has long been dominated by two main political parties. The KDP, founded by the Barzani family in the 1940s, has a largely tribal orientation. The Patriotic Union of Kurdistan (PUK), founded by Jalal Talabani and other dissidents from the KDP in 1975, has a generally leftist ideological orientation (although it also relies on a tribal support base). The long-standing political rivalry between the two parties has been punctuated both by periods of open warfare and by occasional cooperation against the Iraqi state. A great deal of political power also rests with tribal chiefs, whose fighting forces—known as the *jash*—serve as a sort of auxiliary force of the Iraqi military.[19]

Demands for Kurdish independence from Iraq—or at least autonomy—date back nearly a century or more. A series of revolts in the 1960s escalated to open war against the state by the end of the decade. Despite Iranian backing of the Kurds (and a nearly successful settlement in 1970 that was blocked only by disagreement over the status of the city of Kirkuk), the uprising was brutally crushed by the Iraqi military in 1975. Two hundred thousand Kurdish refugees fled to neighboring Iran, and the regime razed over eighteen hundred villages, forcibly displacing more than six hundred thousand people to "collective villages." In an attempt to break Kurdish communal cohesion, Arabs were encouraged to marry Kurdish women, while many Kurds were fired from academic and government jobs or transferred out of Iraqi Kurdistan.[20]

Under the pretext that Kurds were acting as Iranian agents in the Iran-Iraq War, the Iraqi regime launched a genocidal campaign against them in 1988. Under the leadership of Saddam Hussein's cousin Ali Hassan al-Majid (later known as "Chemical Ali"), hundreds of villages were destroyed. Men were rounded up and executed, while women and children were held in concentration camps, where many died. The survivors were transferred to resettlement towns elsewhere in the Kurdish region of Iraq (often far from the border with Iran).[21]

However, in the aftermath of the Gulf War in 1991 the Kurds experienced an unprecedented degree of autonomy. The rivalry between the KDP and the PUK remained as intense as ever, leading to four years of civil war in the mid-1990s. The two managed to find a degree of political equilibrium following the American invasion of Iraq in 2003, and for the past decade Iraqi Kurdistan has enjoyed both autonomy and strong economic growth fueled by the oil industry. Kurdish institutions—in both government and civil society—have strengthened. And despite an aggressive military response by the Iraqi government to a referendum in September 2017 on the question of independence—leading to the loss of Kurdish control over Kirkuk—Iraqi Kurdistan retains a great deal of autonomy.

There are clearly some commonalities across all three regions. The Turkish, Iraqi, and Syrian regimes have all, at various times and to various degrees, viewed Kurdish nationalism as a threat to their respective ethno-national political projects. All three Kurdish communities have experienced state violence and have responded with nationalist mobilization, sometimes in the form of armed uprisings. But significant differences in the nature and ideology of the organizations remain. One of the most significant is the very different roles that women play in the armed factions in Iraq versus Syria and Turkey.

Women in the Kurdish Forces

The PKK in Turkey

The PKK places unusual emphasis on women's empowerment, both as a political position and as a matter of internal policy. The liberation of women constitutes a core tenet of the PKK's ideology and a central component of the political education received by all fighters (both men and women). Women have been part of the PKK since it was founded in 1978; its founding members included Sakine Cansiz, who was assassinated in Paris in 2013, and Kesire Yildirim, who was once married to Abdullah Öcalan.[22] Today, by PKK policy all political leadership positions must be held jointly by a man and a woman.[23]

Perhaps even more unusual is that this emphasis on gender parity is also reflected in the PKK's military wing. In the late 1980s and 1990s the organization's armed wing began accepting large numbers of female recruits, and today roughly 40 percent of the organization's fighters are women. Men and women largely fight in integrated military units. This sets the PKK apart from many leftist militant groups that have female auxiliary units or separate (and often much smaller) female combat units. Because women's integration into the PKK's military structure also extends to the officer corps, male soldiers sometimes find themselves taking orders from female officers—a rare state of affairs among both state and nonstate military forces in the Middle East.

This arrangement is not entirely frictionless. One former PKK commander described her soldiers occasionally complaining about taking orders from a woman or questioning her ability to carry out difficult tasks. She recounted:

> For example, you basically share the same conditions. You walk together, you eat together, you sleep together. You live the same difficulty as him, if there is any difficulty. Even though they do not reflect it to you in practice, in his head they see you as second place. Let's say that I am the commander of the operation and we are going to some place together. I have five or six fighters on my command. A few of them are good at using arms. And I

command this group. If the operation fails and we are ambushed . . . [and] I am telling them to withdraw, they do not obey me. They cannot digest a woman to be their commander, they cannot accept a woman's authority easily. Or when they make a wrong decision and you tell it to them, they go on saying, "See, she's a woman, so she is acting with maternal emotions." The most obvious example was this: it was winter and there was snow up to here [gesturing to her chest]. So men and women had to go get flour for making bread and they would carry [the bags] on their backs. Some women got more weight than men. But those who were ill like me could not carry that much. Men started to make fun of us right away. Maybe they were joking but there was a conception behind that, for sure. We were equal in [the] fight because we were sacrificing a lot. If they were lying on the floor, we were also lying on the floor. If they were fighting, we were fighting likewise. In appearance, there was equality. But their conception did not change.[24]

One male former member of the PKK explained the dynamic as follows: "Most of the people who came to the PKK were from the villages. They didn't have a good education, or no education. They had a feudal view of women. Like [the previous interview subject] said, they didn't take them seriously, they didn't listen to them and kind of insulted, made fun of them. Also they wanted to take their place."[25]

These complaints are not substantially more severe than those recounted by female officers in the American military, and in some cases far less so.[26] Nevertheless, they do reflect a broader theme in interviews with Kurdish female activists, who describe a "double struggle," both against the Turkish state and against Kurdish men. One activist explained this dynamic as follows:

The dual violence that we face both from the male-hegemonic mentality and the state brought us to this struggle. And this gives us an immense sense of self-confidence that we're able to express ourselves as women, do politics as women, taking part in the struggle as women. Because we faced such significant violence from the state, we continue our struggle to empower and support women, create safe spaces and life spaces for them who have also endured male violence.[27]

In the past the PKK made a number of concessions, large and small, to prevailing gender norms. One party activist described a former policy under which female soldiers were not allowed to smoke in front of male soldiers (this was eventually overturned).[28] A long-standing ban on sexual or romantic relationships between male and female soldiers (or between soldiers and civilians) was intended, at least in part, to reassure families that their daughters would not be morally compromised by joining the PKK.[29] However, these concessions were fairly minor compared to the organization's broad acceptance—and encouragement—of women's participation in its military wing.

The Syrian Kurdish Forces

The Syrian Kurdish armed groups are similar to the PKK's armed forces in many ways. Ideologically, the PYD (the political party of which the YPG and YPJ are the armed wings) also explicitly advocates women's empowerment. As in the PKK, all political roles in the PYD are held jointly by a man and a woman, and a significant portion of Syrian Kurdish fighters are women. The two parallel armed forces—the all-male YPG and the all-female YPJ—together comprise as many as sixty thousand fighters, of whom roughly twenty-four thousand are female (although precise numbers are difficult to find).[30]

The organization derives its roots from smaller armed groups formed in the early 2000s as a military wing of the PYD (and in alliance with the PKK) after the collapse of the alliance between the PKK and the Syrian state and the corresponding increase in state repression against Syrian Kurds. With the emergence of ISIS as a threat to Kurdish territory in 2013, these groups were reconstituted into the much-larger YPG, whose command staff initially included both men and women. The arrival of female PKK combat veterans in 2013 led to the formation of a separate female fighting force, officially established on April 4, 2013.[31] Today the YPJ and the YPG act as parallel military forces under the political command of the PYD and the broader military umbrella of the SDF. Although the SDF does include other armed factions, the YPG and YPJ form the military backbone of the US-backed alliance.[32]

Like the PKK, the PYD has explicitly encouraged the recruitment of female soldiers. They have also established a female officer corps, although the existing division between the YPG and the YPJ means that female officers largely command female troops. Women interviewed in propaganda videos produced by the YPG media office describe their motives for joining the YPJ in terms that echo the PKK's ideology. One fighter interviewed says that she "joined the YPJ to take revenge for our martyred friends, to carry on their resistance, and to fight the injustice on [*sic*] women."[33] Another states, "I joined to protect the rights of women and to carry on the resistance of our martyrs."[34] And a third, a commander named Azima, explains: "We didn't only organize ourselves against ISIS, but against the conditions previously imposed by our society. So there was a struggle against this as well."[35] Moreover, people critical of the SDF generally, and of the YPJ more specifically, allege that fighters are drafted against their will, including female fighters and boys and girls under the age of eighteen.[36] This suggests that the YPJ's egalitarianism also extends to its more coercive behavior, such as forced recruitment.

The Iraqi Peshmerga

The Iraqi peshmerga are very different than the PKK and the YPJ regarding the involvement of women in their fighting forces. Historically neither the PUK nor the KDP have prioritized the recruitment of female soldiers. A women's peshmerga unit was established by the PUK in 1996 but remained quite small, including only about five to six hundred fighters, in comparison to as many as one hundred thousand male fighters. By 2015 budget shortfalls had led the Kurdish Regional Government (the de facto government of the Iraqi Kurdish region) to halt the recruitment of female fighters entirely, despite high levels of interest from women in joining.[37] As of 2016 some one thousand women were being trained for the Zeravani, the peshmerga's military police.[38] But this is a far cry from the much larger proportion of female fighters in the Kurdish forces in Syria and Turkey.

Despite the much smaller number of women serving in the peshmerga as compared to other Kurdish armed factions, the Kurdish Regional Government has still tapped into the trope of the glorified Kurdish female fighter battling ISIS to promote the image of Iraqi Kurdistan as a modern, secular, stable, and pro-American place at least in part to attract foreign investment.[39] The success of this effort is reflected in reporting by Western media that conflates all Kurdish forces and even in cultural products associated with Iraqi Kurdistan. For example, music videos by the Iraqi Kurdish singer Helly Luv feature her in a jumpsuit somewhat resembling combat fatigues and gold high-heeled shoes, lobbing Molotov cocktails and leading crowds of Kurds against a military foe vaguely similar to ISIS.[40] But the image of the liberated female Kurdish soldier fighting as part of an egalitarian armed group does not reflect the reality of the Iraqi Kurdish forces; rather, it is more reflective of the Kurdish forces in Turkey and Syria.[41] This variation in the roles of women among the three sets of Kurdish armed forces presents an interesting puzzle. Why are there so many female fighters in the Turkish and Syrian Kurdish forces but so few in the Iraqi ones?

Explaining Variation in Women's Participation

The best explanation for the variation in the participation of female combatants across the various Kurdish groups lies in two interrelated facets of these organizations' respective processes of political mobilization: their very different ideologies and their different positions relative to existing Kurdish elites. The ideological differences are perhaps the more obvious of these two issues. The PKK and its allied groups, including both the PYD in Syria and the Iranian PJAK (Partiya Jiyana Azad a Kurdistanê, the Kurdistan Free Life Party) look to Öcalan (referred to by movement members as "Apo," or "uncle") as their ideological guide. The movement's ideological program has evolved over time, from a focus on more traditional Marxism in the movement's earlier years to the embrace of "democratic confederalism" in the early 2000s. Despite this ideological evolution, however, an explicit focus on women's rights has remained a prominent feature of the PKK's ideology; indeed, it has arguably become more central over time as the number of women in the organization has increased.[42] This includes an explicit commitment to equality between women and men both within the organization and in society more broadly, as well as an explicit rejection of patriarchal gender norms. The empowerment of women within Kurdish society—including an end to domestic violence, greater access to education for women, and a shift in social attitudes overall—has been central to many of the PKK's social policies as well as those advocated by its allies in civil society and by its political fellow travelers.[43]

The Iraqi Kurdish factions' respective ideological frameworks are quite different. While at least in theory the KDP was loosely leftist in its early years, in practice it was largely defined by tribal loyalties and patrimonialism. The PUK was somewhat more ideological, adhering to generally leftist principles and at various points making common cause with the Iraqi Communist Party, but it was never as intensely ideological as the PKK. More important, neither organization ever articulated a specific commitment to women's rights or framed gender egalitarianism as a central ideological feature of its political platform.

In addition, the political contexts faced by each of these groups were very different, particularly with regard to local political competition. The PKK's leftist ideology, while perhaps sincere in its own right, emerged in the context of a wider leftist challenge to Kemalist nationalism in Turkey as represented by the Cumhuriyet Halk Partisi (Republican People's Party). By embracing a Marxist-Leninist ideology, the PKK sought not only to mobilize the Kurdish public in the cause of Kurdish self-determination but also to both distinguish itself from and directly challenge the dominant ideology of the Turkish state and the Turkish state-building project as a whole. Kemalist secularism had not, overall, led to significant changes in the daily lives of rural Kurdish women, which left an ideological opening for the doctrine advocated by the PKK.[44] Moreover, the Turkish state was not the PKK's only rival. Even as it challenged the authority of the state, it did so largely without reliance on the local tribal chieftains or other rural political elites for legitimacy. The PKK's early leadership included a number of urban intellectuals; Öcalan himself became politicized as a student in Ankara.[45] When the PKK was founded and launched its insurgency in the southeast, it was far less politically beholden to rural elites than the KPD had been in Iraq.

In combination this meant that early on the PKK was ideologically predisposed to recruiting women and largely unrestrained from doing so because it did not need to appease conservative rural community leaders. These permissive factors combined to facilitate the inclusion of large numbers of women who became politicized in the early 1990s as a result of the military crackdown in the Kurdish regions of Turkey, including women who found themselves politicized by the experience of advocating for their imprisoned husbands and sons, sometimes in the context of demonstrations outside Diyarbakir prison. Some of these women found their way into the Kurdish national movement and in some cases joined the military wing of the party. They were joined by increasing numbers of young rural women seeking greater personal autonomy and an alternative to early marriage and urban women who had been radicalized as university students. As women joined in greater numbers, they sharpened the PKK's focus on women's liberation from within the organization.[46]

This focus on women's liberation was then extended to the Syrian forces. While the nature of elite competition in Syria was different, by the time the PYD was formed in 2004 women's participation was almost a given. The inclusion of female combatants had by then become a core characteristic of the PKK, which served as a parent organization in the PYD's early years and whose ideological and organizational character were therefore reflected in the Syrian Kurdish movement.

There are arguably also practical reasons for the inclusion of female combatants: because the YPG drew at least in part on PKK fighters of Syrian origin for recruits in the early days of the war against ISIS, the nature of the PKK meant that, almost by definition, some of those veteran fighters were women. (Indeed, these fighters formed the core of the YPJ when it was first established.)[47] Even if the Syrian Kurdish leadership had sought to distance itself from the PKK's egalitarian recruitment practices for domestic political reasons, it would have been militarily foolhardy to do so, as it would have meant turning away fighters who represented a critically important resource.

However, the situation of Kurdish armed groups in Iraq was quite different. While the relatively diverse nature of the PKK's recruitment base and strong ideological core meant that it did not, for the most part, have to rely on tribal elites for legitimacy or authority, the PUK and especially the KDP derived their power and legitimacy from those very networks. The KDP in particular repeatedly retreated from explicitly nationalist or progressive political objectives in the 1970s in order to preserve the power of both the Barzani clan and its tribal allies. At the same time, many of the most direct challenges to the Barzanis' power, particularly in the 1970s, came from tribal rivals. Even the rivalry between the KDP and PUK was strongly shaped by the rivalry between the Barzanis and Talabanis.[48] Neither set of leaders was invested in entirely uprooting the existing norms and power relations that characterized rural Kurdish society in Iraq, because it was these norms on which their own power bases were built. Moreover, neither adhered to the sort of radical leftist doctrine embraced by the PKK.

In Iraq, leftist politics were closely aligned with Arab nationalism, a doctrine that prioritized Arab identity as the basis for political mobilization. This represented a direct challenge to Kurdish nationalism in the Iraqi context. Despite the long history of Kurdish membership in the Iraqi Communist Party, the pan-Arab focus of the Iraqi left often served as a barrier to creating a strong ideological alliance from the perspective of the Kurdish parties. The incentives to embrace leftist (and feminist) politics as a means of challenging the dominant state narrative that existed in Turkey were not present for the Kurdish parties in Iraq. Instead, there were clear incentives to maintain the status quo.

Conclusions

The choice to include—or reject—large numbers of women in a nonstate armed movement can have a range of consequences for the group itself, for its associated political parties, and perhaps for society more broadly. Comparison between the Iraqi Kurdish factions and those in Turkey and Syria is instructive in this regard.

One consequence of recruiting women can be that, once present, they increase the organization's ideological focus on women's rights and women's liberation. This dynamic presents something of a chicken-and-egg problem: there is evidence that a movement that is more prone to emphasizing women's rights, or even one that is not opposed to them, is likely to recruit more women in the first place.[49] But some interview subjects suggested that the PKK's ideological focus on women's rights was actually *increased* by the presence of women in the organization: "In the beginning, it was different than it is today. As more women joined the PKK, there was more and more discussion of gender issues. From the beginning there were women recruits, but the PKK was a military and male-dominant organization. It was women's participation that changed it into a feminist organization."[50]

What about the question of military effectiveness? Are militant groups that recruit large numbers of women more or less effective than those that do not? Effectiveness is difficult to measure, even with regard to the various Kurdish militant groups, because all three have had mixed battlefield records and mostly for reasons that have nothing to do with the gender composition of their fighting forces. In Iraq the almost entirely male KDP and PUK have been historically hampered by their antagonism for one another and by the resulting intra-Kurdish armed conflicts. There is little reason to think that this problem would have been lessened by the inclusion of women in their ranks.

The PKK, with its mixed units, has been effective at creating instability and challenging Turkish state authority in the Kurdish regions of Turkey but has had limited success in securing any meaningful territorial gains, even before its objectives shifted from an independent Kurdistan to regional autonomy in the early 2000s. There is little evidence that the use of mixed-gender military units shaped this overall outcome or that the PKK would have been any more or less effective had it used only male soldiers. One position that has been filled primarily by women is that of suicide bomber. In the 1990s there were fifteen suicide attacks by the PKK, eleven of which were carried out by women.[51] Though these attacks were largely operationally successful (in that they produced casualties), suicide attacks represent a relatively small portion of the PKK's overall operations, so it is reasonable to question what sort of positive impact they had on the PKK's overall objectives.

Meanwhile, the Syrian Kurdish all-female YPJ has fought alongside the all-male YPG, participating in key ways in a number of successful and strategically important missions, such as the defense of the town of Kobane against a takeover by ISIS. Azima, a commander in the YPJ, described the importance of the battle at Kobane in a propaganda video released by the YPG:

> I was wondering how much women would really protect their land. How much they would love it, how much they would struggle for it. Those were questions during the battle[s] of Sarikani, Mabruka, Rawiya, Til Kocher, until the battle of Kobane, and the last one in Manbij. The role that women played left its fingerprint on history. For example, in the war of Kobane, of all the fighters, 80 percent were women. From the coordination team to the units on the front line, there were women. The idea that if there are women ISIS won't go to paradise, that if women kill them they would go to hell— this is not true. It isn't true because ISIS attacked us, sending a lot of their men. For example, they would send 250 terrorists for 30 of our comrades. We have an expression: "You ruin them." We ruin their plans, their tactics, their goals, their existence. The victory of Kobane was epic, and with the participation of women it became heroic.[52]

There is some reason to believe that organizations that recruit women may end up with better fighters from the start. Simple math suggests that an organization that is able to draw fighters from 100 percent of the available fighting age population can be more selective about who it recruits than an organization limited to only 50 percent of the same population. It will therefore end up with a better quality of soldier, or at least with soldiers who are more ideologically committed. Such recruits are likely to be both more effective and less brutal toward the civilian population than those motivated by more material concerns, such as the chance to loot.[53] The PKK, as an organization with a strongly defined ideological core, had a powerful incentive to recruit fighters who were receptive to the movement's ideology and willing to go through its lengthy indoctrination process.

Being able to recruit more selectively was clearly an advantage in this regard.[54] But this logic can, of course, cut both ways: women who join a militant group to escape early marriage or to pursue a degree of personal autonomy not available to them in their civilian lives are perhaps less likely to be ideologically motivated than those joining a movement for purely political reasons.

Finally, women's participation in armed movements can have an impact well outside the groups themselves. Women's involvement in militant groups can lead to greater roles for women politically. The PYD in Syria has a rule that each political position must be held jointly by a man and a woman, which automatically puts a number of women in powerful political positions. One example is Ilham Ahmed, one of the two co-chairs of the Syrian Democratic Council (the political wing of the SDF), who has been an outspoken advocate for the Syrian Kurdish cause.[55] One YPJ commander interviewed for a propaganda video drew a clear connection between the existence of the YPJ and changes in the role of women in society: "Today, because of the YPJ, women take part in all institutions of Rojava. They play their own role in media, health, economy, art and culture, language training, in every field. The fact that today women are building their own place in society is a victory won by the blood of YPJ martyrs."[56]

In Turkey the PKK has a quota system for filling political positions within the organization, while the main Kurdish civilian political party in Turkey (which is not affiliated with the PKK but which is certainly ideologically linked to the organization) has a 40 percent quota system for women in its electoral lists and parliamentary delegation. There is, again, a chicken-and-egg problem here: perhaps these organizations were more predisposed to recruit women in the first place because they were ideologically committed to gender equality. But in the case of the PKK and its civilian political fellow travelers, the shift toward greater inclusion of women has taken place over time and has increased as more women have joined. The early leadership of the movement did include women, but they were greatly outnumbered by men. Moreover, some of the political activists interviewed described having to struggle within the Kurdish movement to ensure that women's voices were heard and women's issues were prioritized.[57]

It is worth noting that the lack of women in the peshmerga has not translated into an absence of women in politics in Iraqi Kurdistan, where there is a 30 percent quota for women in the Kurdish National Assembly (the Kurdish regional legislature); this is higher than the 25 percent quota in place in the rest of Iraq.[58] This suggests that women's participation in armed groups can certainly shape the policies pursued by the political wings of those organizations, but it does not necessarily mean that this is the only route by which women's involvement can occur.

In sum, the following are our main findings:

- Women's participation in the Kurdish movements in Iraq, Syria, and Turkey varies a great deal, from high levels of participation in Syria and Turkey to lower levels in Iraq.
- Variation in women's participation is shaped both by ideology and by the constraints (or absence thereof) resulting from the organizations' relations with traditional elites.
- Women's participation changes armed movements from within. Those policy changes can in turn have wider political and social consequences.

At present the political situations in Syria, Turkey, and Iraq are very much in flux. The PKK remains in conflict with the Turkish state, while its civilian political allies face increased repression. In Iraq, a 2017 referendum held in the Kurdish regions on the question of independence led to a military crackdown by the Iraqi state, and internal rivalries continue among the main political parties and their respective armed wings. The Kurdish-held territories in Syria face increasing threats to their security and autonomy from the Turkish military. Should a Kurdish polity be established on territory in any of these three states, it will be interesting to see how women's roles in the armed political movements that have fought for Kurdish independence shape their political roles in any future Kurdish state.

Notes

Epigraph: YPJ Kurdish Female Fighters: A Day in Syria, YouTube video, 24:59, posted by Eleftheria, October 23, 2014, https://www.youtube.com/watch?v=7Vhh_zGzEb4. Translation taken from the video's subtitles.

1. Dilar Dirik, "Western Fascination with 'Badass' Kurdish Women," Al Jazeera, October 29, 2014, http://www.aljazeera.com/indepth/opinion/2014/10/western-fascination-with-badas-2014102112410527736.html; Mohammed A. Salih, "Meet the Badass Women Fighting the Islamic State," *Foreign Policy*, September 12, 2014, https://foreignpolicy.com/2014/09/12/meet-the-badass-women

-fighting-the-islamic-state/; "Meet the Badass Peshmerga Women," *Full Frontal with Samantha Bee*, August 9, 2017, produced by Razan Ghalayini.

2. Elizabeth McLaughlin, "Women at War: Meet the Female Peshmerga Fighters Taking on ISIS," *ABC News*, May 16, 2016, https://abcnews.go.com/Inter national/women-war-meet-female-peshmerga-fighters-taking-isis/story?id=39 142160.

3. Most media sources put the proportion of women in the PKK at about 40 percent. Haidar Khezri, "Kurdish Troops Fight for Freedom—and Women's Equality—on Battlegrounds across Middle East," *The Conversation*, March 19, 2018, http://theconversation.com/kurdish-troops-fight-for-freedom-and -womens-equality-on-battlegrounds-across-middle-east-91364; "Female Fighting Force of the PKK," *BBC News*, January 5, 2014, http://www.bbc.com/news/av /world-middle-east-25610424/who-are-the-female-fighters-of-the-pkk. This number is echoed by some academic sources as well, including Vera Eccarius-Kelly, *The Militant Kurds: A Dual Strategy for Freedom* (Santa Barbara, CA: Praeger, 2011). Nevertheless, this figure has been contested. Based on casualty data, Güneş Murat Tezcür has argued that the number is probably closer to 16 percent. See Tezcür, "Ordinary People, Extraordinary Risks: Participation in an Ethnic Rebellion," *American Political Science Review* 110, no. 2 (2016): 247–64, doi:10.1017/s00030 55416000150.

4. Eccarius-Kelly, *Militant Kurds*; Aliza Marcus, *Blood and Belief: The PKK and the Kurdish Fight for Independence* (New York: New York University Press, 2007).

5. Interview with S.C., writer. All interview subjects are referred to using their initials. All interviews were originally conducted in Turkish (through an interpreter) and translated into English.

6. Marcus, *Blood and Belief*, 222.

7. Murray Bookchin, *The Ecology of Freedom: The Emergence and Dissolution of Hierarchy* (Palo Alto, CA: Cheshire, 1982); Murray Bookchin and Janet Biehl, *The Modern Crisis* (Montreal: Black Rose, 1987); Murray Bookchin, *Remaking Society: Pathways to a Green Future* (New York: South End, 1990).

8. The PKK is not the only Kurdish political force in Turkey. At present the major nonviolent Kurdish political party is the Halkların Demokratik Partisi (HDP), or People's Democratic Party. It received 13 percent of the seats in the Turkish Parliament in the 2015 elections. As of this writing much of the HDP's leadership, including its former co-presidents Figen Yuksekdag and Selahattin Demirtas, has been jailed.

9. For more on the history of the PKK, see Marcus, *Blood and Belief*; Ali Kemal Ozcan, *Turkey's Kurds: A Theoretical Analysis of the PKK and Abdullah Öcalan* (New York: Routledge, 2006).

10. "Turkey-PKK Conflict: Scores Dead in Clashes in Southeast," *BBC News*, January 27, 2016, https://www.bbc.com/news/world-europe-35424525.

11. Harriet Allsopp, *The Kurds of Syria: Political Parties and Identity in the Middle East* (London: I. B. Tauris, 2015), 86; Michael M. Gunter, *Out of Nowhere: The Kurds of Syria in Peace and War* (London: Hurst, 2014), 10.

12. Allsopp, *Kurds of Syria*, 73–98; Gunter, *Out of Nowhere*, 17.

13. Gunter, *Out of Nowhere*, 21.

14. Allsopp, *Kurds of Syria*.

15. A similar party was established in Iran in 2004. It was known as PJAK, or Kurdistan Free Life Party.

16. Allsopp, *Kurds of Syria*, 103–4.

17. Gunter, *Out of Nowhere*, 30.

18. As of this writing, one of these three cantons, Afrin, is under Turkish military control.

19. For more on the history of the Kurds of Iraq, see David McDowall, *A Modern History of the Kurds*, 3rd ed. (London: I. B. Tauris, 2004); and David Romano, *The Kurdish Nationalist Movement: Opportunity, Mobilization and Identity* (Cambridge: Cambridge University Press, 2006).

20. McDowall, *Modern History of the Kurds*, 338–40.

21. McDowall, *Modern History of the Kurds*, 365.

22. Constanze Letsch, "Sakine Cansiz: 'A Legend among PKK Members,'" *Guardian*, January 10, 2013, http://www.theguardian.com/world/2013/jan/10/sakine-cansiz-pkk-kurdish-activist.

23. This practice extends to the leadership of the HDP. The empowerment of women within the HDP is a consistent theme in interviews conducted with HDP members.

24. Interview with A.C., political activist.

25. Interview with Z.

26. Paula Broadwell and Kate Hendricks Thomas, "The Marines' Naked-Photo Scandal Shows Military Culture Is Still Sexist," *Washington Post*, March 7, 2017, https://www.washingtonpost.com/posteverything/wp/2017/03/07/the-marines-naked-photo-scandal-shows-military-culture-is-still-sexist/; Talya Minsberg, "Women Describe Their Struggles with Gender Roles in Military," *New York Times*, May 24, 2015, https://www.nytimes.com/2015/05/25/health/women-describe-their-struggles-with-gender-roles-in-military.html.

27. Interview with I., HDP district party official.

28. Interview with M., HDP official.

29. Interview with E.K., human rights advocate. See also Marcus, *Blood and Belief*, 198.

30. Tom Perry, "Exclusive: Syrian Kurdish YPG Aims to Expand Force to over 100,000," Reuters, March 20, 2017, https://www.reuters.com/article/us-mideast-crisis-syria-ypg-exclusive/exclusive-syrian-kurdish-ypg-aims-to-expand-force-to-over-100000-idUSKBN16R1QS.

31. Michael Knapp, Anja Flach, and Ercan Ayboga, *Revolution in Rojava: Democratic Autonomy and Women's Liberation in Syrian Kurdistan*, trans. Janet Biehl (London: Pluto, 2016), 133–36; *YPJ: Women's Defense Units (Women's Protection Units)—English/Kurdî*, YouTube video, 17:06, posted by YPG Press Office, September 25, 2016, https://www.youtube.com/watch?v=_OWQ-apZC78.

32. The SDF was branded as such in part to distance the YPG/J from the PKK and in order to make it more politically palatable for the United States to offer its support to the Kurdish forces against ISIS. The SDF also includes Sunni Arab fighters and Yazidi and Assyrian Christian units. Some of the latter include female fighters. Pascal Andresen, "In This Sign They Will Conquer?—Christian Militias in the Syrian Conflict," *Bellingcat*, November 4, 2017, https://www.bellingcat.com/news/mena/2017/11/04/sign-will-conquer-christian-militias-syrian-conflict/; Luke Mogelson, "Dark Victory in Raqqa," *New Yorker*, October 30, 2017, https://www.newyorker.com/magazine/2017/11/06/dark-victory-in-raqqa.

33. *YPJ: Women's Defense Units*.

34. *YPJ: Women's Defense Units*.

35. *YPJ: Women's Defense Units*.

36. "Syria: Kurdish Forces Violating Child Soldier Ban," Human Rights Watch, July 15, 2015, https://www.hrw.org/news/2015/07/10/syria-kurdish-forces-violating-child-soldier-ban-0.

37. "KRG Halts Recruiting of Female Peshmerga," *Rudaw*, June 22, 2015, http://www.rudaw.net/english/kurdistan/220620151.

38. McLaughlin, "Women at War."

39. Nicholas S. Glastonbury, "Building Brand Kurdistan: Helly Luv, the Gender of Nationhood, and the War on Terror," *Kurdish Studies* 6, no. 1 (May 2018): 121–22, https://journal.tplondon.com/index.php/ks/article/view/1050/701.

40. Glastonbury, "Building Brand Kurdistan"; *Helly Luv—Revolution*, YouTube video, 7:19, posted by HellyLuvVEVO, May 28, 2015, https://www.youtube.com/watch?v=fLMtTQsiW6I.

41. Glastonbury, "Building Brand Kurdistan," 116.

42. Marcus, *Blood and Belief*, 173.

43. Interviews with I. and M.

44. Metin Yüksel, "The Encounter of Kurdish Women with Nationalism in Turkey," *Middle Eastern Studies* 42, no. 5 (2006): 777–802, doi: 10.1080/00263200600828022.

45. Marcus, *Blood and Belief*, 25–31.

46. Ora Szekely, "Fighting about Women: Ideologies of Gender in the Syrian Civil War," *Journal of Global Security Studies* (forthcoming).

47. Knapp, Flach, and Ayboga, *Revolution in Rojava*, 136.

48. McDowall, *Modern History of the Kurds*, 320–30. See also Romano, *The Kurdish National Movement*.

49. Reed M. Wood and Jakana L. Thomas, "Women on the Frontline: Rebel Group Ideology and Women's Participation in Violent Rebellion," *Journal of Peace Research* 54, no. 1 (2017): 31–46, doi: 10.1177/0022343316675025.

50. Interview with E.K.

51. Zeynep Sahin-Mencutek, "Strong in the Movement, Strong in the Party: Women's Representation in the Kurdish Party of Turkey," *Political Studies* 64, no. 2 (2016): 480–81, doi: 10.1111/1467–9248.12188. See also Mia Bloom, *Bombshell: Women and Terrorism* (Philadelphia: University of Pennsylvania Press, 2012).

52. *#YPJ Fighters from Deir al-Zour Frontline Speak on Their Participation*, YouTube video, 1:47, posted by YPG Press Office, May 11, 2018, https://www .youtube.com/watch?v=68ngu-nXSB0. Note: the quotations included from this source are transcribed from the subtitles in the video.

53. Jeremy Weinstein, *Inside Rebellion: The Politics of Insurgent Violence* (Cambridge: Cambridge University Press, 2006).

54. Marcus, *Blood and Belief.*

55. Ilham Ahmed, "The Young Feminist Who Died for My People," *New York Times*, March 21, 2018, https://www.nytimes.com/2018/03/21/opinion/anna -campbell-kurds-syria.html; Ilham Ahmed, "We're America's Best Friend in Syria. Turkey Bombed Us Anyway," *Washington Post*, April 28, 2017, https://www.wash ingtonpost.com/news/democracy-post/wp/2017/04/28/were-americas-best -friend-in-syria-turkey-bombed-us-anyway/.

56. *#YPJ Fighters from Deir al-Zour Frontline.*

57. Interviews with I. and B., activists.

58. "The Kurdistan Parliament," Kurdistan Regional Government, 2018, http://cabinet.gov.krd/p/p.aspx?l=12&p=229.

3

Colombia

Women Waging War and Peace

We chose a female comrade to represent us because we thought the thing that could hurt this macho bourgeoisie the most would be to send them a woman . . . they knew we had men and women in our command and they hoped to negotiate with a man . . . We sent them a woman so they would see what they were in for.
—COMANDANTE UNO AKA ROSEMBERG PABÓN, FORMER M-19 COMBATANT

The conclusion of a peace accord in 2016 between the Colombian government and the largest insurgent group operating in the country, the Fuerzas Armadas Revolucionarias de Colombia (Revolutionary Armed Forces of Colombia, or FARC), was rightfully hailed as a landmark achievement. Claims that the accord meant the end of all active armed conflict in the Western Hemisphere were hyperbolic, but the agreement was the result of a five-year process that succeeded where many previous efforts had failed.[1] Peace negotiations conducted in Havana were also unique in the degree to which they included women. The Gender Subcommission, an official body at the talks, consisted of women representing the national government, the armed forces, and the FARC. Its work—which drew on the testimony of thousands of women impacted by the conflict—was hailed by UN leadership as "a unique mechanism in the history of conflict resolution."[2]

The significance of gender mainstreaming in Colombia's peace process[3]—in a world where peace negotiations generally suffer from an underrepresentation of women and particularly women representing armed groups—cannot be overlooked.[4] Yet it should not be surprising that this particular case was a watershed, given the long history of women's engagement with the FARC and other armed groups in the Colombian conflict.

Since the 1960s the FARC has advocated for the rights of rural poor Colombians. Over time it has also adopted into its platform goals in favor of rights for indigenous groups, women, and, more recently, the LGBTQ population within Colombia. At the start of the twenty-first century an estimated 30 to 40 percent of the FARC's fighting force was female. However, the number of total fighters in the organization has dwindled significantly—from an estimated twenty thousand in 2000 to about seven thousand in 2016.[5] Compare this to the membership numbers of Ejército de Liberación Nacional (National Liberation Army, or ELN), another leftist group that is smaller but nonetheless benefits from a substantial female cohort. The ELN—which also has been engaged in armed struggle against the Colombian state since the 1960s but which has *not* reached an accord with the government—is believed to have about fifteen hundred to two thousand troops. This likewise represents a declining membership over time as a result of a sustained anti-insurgency campaign by the Colombian government and paramilitary groups.[6] Still, women are believed to make up about 25 percent of ELN's total force.[7]

The history of female fighters in Colombia has included substantial participation by women in several armed groups that were initially active alongside the FARC and the ELN but that disarmed during the 1990s and early 2000s. These include the leftist-nationalist 19th of April Movement (M-19), itself a splinter group of the FARC; the Marxist Ejército Popular de Liberación (Popular Liberation Army, or EPL);[8] and the right-wing paramilitary Autodefensas Unidas de Colombia (United Self-Defense Forces of Colombia, or AUC). At the time of disarmament the EPL and M-19 each numbered about one to two thousand fighters, with roughly 25 percent of disarmed combatants being women.[9] Between 2003 and 2012 the Colombian government demobilized 35,314 individuals from the AUC, about 7 percent of whom were women.[10]

This chapter offers an overview of how women have been mobilized in the FARC and the ELN. Given the long-standing history of these two groups, we pay particular attention to exploring how mobilization processes have evolved. Specifically, our analysis shows that women became more engaged and strategically important to the FARC over time, eventually culminating in the highly visible presence of women as negotiators during the Havana talks. Over time there has also been an ideological evolution among armed groups on the Colombian left regarding gender rights and LGBTQ rights that coincides with the growing importance of women in the conflict. We argue that this evolution is a by-product, rather than a cause, of the engagement and advancement of women within these groups. It appears that various armed groups (at least on the left) have emulated one another in ideological development, in strategies related to the use of women, and in the inclusion of women in peace talks. These coincident evolutions suggest a dynamic of "outbidding" among these groups.

Marxism, Nationalism, and Feminism in Colombia

While the FARC's emphasis on women's rights was at the center of its agenda during talks in Havana, women's empowerment has not always been an issue central to its platform. In fact, early communiqués by the FARC laying out its political agenda make no reference to gender issues at all.[11] Among the early policy demands advanced by the FARC were agrarian reform, financial assistance from the government for poor farmers, and the protection of and allocation of financial resources to indigenous communities.[12] Some historians have described the organization itself during this early phase as a peasant self-defense organization lacking a formal hierarchy.[13] Other FARC documents from the 1960s also decry the presence of American military installations in Colombia.[14]

The organization grew and changed significantly during the period between about 1970 and 1982. With the expansion of commercial agriculture and subsequent displacement of more peasants in rural Colombia, the FARC's ranks swelled. This growth necessitated organizational change, and the FARC established a military-style hierarchy—complete with rules of conduct—and revisited its political program.[15] While there was some resistance to expanding the role of women in the group at this time, decisions by the FARC at its sixth conference (in 1978) and seventh conference (in 1982) ultimately allowed women to enlist in the newly militarized organization.[16] A declaration in 1985 formally recognized equality among male and female guerrillas, which opened up new opportunities for women in the FARC, including leadership positions.[17]

The FARC's lengthy development of a gender-inclusive ideology contrasts with the evolution of the ELN, which had focused on gender issues much earlier. A 1965 ELN manifesto called on the Colombian government to confer on women their "legitimate rights."[18] One reason for the early discrepancy between these two left-wing organizations, despite claiming similar ideological leanings, may have been that the FARC recruited predominantly

among the peasantry whereas the ELN's recruitment base included intellectuals, students, and Catholics inspired by liberation theology.[19] The ELN
also had ties to the Cuban government and saw itself as situated within the
international context of leftist anticolonial insurgencies.[20] As such, the nod
to women's rights in the group's earliest manifesto was likely an attempt to
situate itself among other contemporary organizations that formed a global
"new left" movement. Contrary to the old left, such organizations—which
often emerged out of student protest movements—viewed themselves as
advocates for broad social change including the liberation of peoples in the
developing world, the dismantling of traditional family structures, and the
rights of women.[21]

Comparing women's engagement within the FARC, the ELN, and other
leftist groups in Colombia suggests that these groups learned from one
another tactically and ideologically. Certainly the existence of many joint
communiqués, open letters, and joint exercises over the years indicates that
Colombia's leftists cooperated when it suited them to do so.[22] The movement of individuals, especially female cadres, between the two groups further suggests some form of organizational learning. Thus, the FARC's
embrace of gender equality in the 1980s was influenced not only by the
presence of women at the margins of its own ranks but also by the engagement of women in other leftist, anticolonial insurgencies in the region and
even worldwide.

Female Fighters in Colombian Armed Groups

Just as the FARC and the ELN followed different evolutionary paths in their
ideologies, they also differ in the circumstances and mechanisms by which
they incorporated women. In the FARC, women's early roles were limited.
Early recruitment practices sometimes mobilized entire families, meaning
that men took up arms while women remained at the margins, performing
services like cooking and caring for children and animals in the camp.
Women also participated in auxiliary groups that supported the FARC
materially and politically.[23]

Women were formally incorporated into the FARC following its 1978
and 1982 conferences, on the condition that they abide by the organization's policies on forced contraception. This policy, which remained in
effect until demobilization, was greatly controversial over the years.
Women in the FARC were not only forced to take measures to prevent
pregnancy but, in the event that they did become pregnant, were also pres-

sured to have abortions or surrender their child to another family. A 2003 report by Human Rights Watch concluded that girls as young as twelve were forced to have contraceptive implants or injections and that teen girls were forced to have abortions.[24] The policy was thus heavily criticized by the state, human rights groups, and the international community.

While the group has denied allegations of forced abortions, it does admit to imposing a pregnancy ban on female cadres and, in some cases, making them leave behind their newborn children.[25] However, the FARC deflected criticism by claiming that it was the realities of war—not malevolence or misogyny—that drove these practices. A 2016 statement by the FARC says, in part, that "a pregnant female combatant means risk of certain death of her and the child she carries," and that women are advised of and agree to the rules on contraception and pregnancy at the time they enlist.[26] FARC members further blame the state for creating conditions that forced them to abandon their children. Wendy Arango, a member of the FARC's peace delegation, said she was forced to leave her newborn son in a hospital because of an "army action" and that officials subsequently refused to grant custody of the child to its grandparents, instead placing the baby in the child welfare system.[27]

These reproductive practices were a catch-22 for FARC women, who often ended up bearing the consequences of the FARC's fairly liberal attitude toward sexual relations. Researchers report that *Farianas* (female FARC cadres) were expected to make themselves available for sexual relationships, though rape was strictly forbidden and women could pick their own partners.[28] While organizational leadership had final approval over sexual relationships, approval was rarely withheld.[29] On the contrary, regular sexual relations (permitted on so-called market days in the camps) were encouraged and may have been used to deter rape or undesirable romantic relationships between combatants and noncombatants in the surrounding communities.[30] At the same time, the FARC seems to have been concerned with preventing sexual relationships within the ranks from becoming serious enough that they might become a distraction or an impetus for defection. In addition to the forced separation and punishment of LGBTQ couples, leadership also intentionally separated some heterosexual couples if their relationships were deemed undesirable.[31]

Beyond sexual partnership, women served a variety of substantive roles in the FARC. For the duration of its armed campaign, women (including girls) occupied some typical support roles, including serving as nurses, radio operators, cooks, and laborers around the camps.[32] However, women also became some of the group's most valued and respected combatants. Natalia Herrera and Douglas Porch found that both the male and female ex-combatants they interviewed said that women were devoted and brave in conflict situations, sometimes more than men. Some of the women they interviewed implied a level of resentment that female cadres fought harder and longer, at times persisting in firefights even after their male companions had retreated.[33]

It is not entirely clear the extent to which these contributions were acknowledged through promotions and advancement. While one study concludes that women held up to 40 percent of midlevel command positions by the time of the Havana talks, other accounts seem to dispute this figure.[34] At the highest levels of the organization, the secretariat was (and still is) composed entirely of men. It is worth noting, however, that Farianas did not seem to harbor any resentment about this gender imbalance. Herrera and Porch suggest that the absence of high-ranking women may have been due to an ambition gap, because many women were content to remain in stereotypically female roles or because they were more concerned with being respected in the positions they held rather than in seeking out opportunities for advancement.[35]

How does women's engagement in the FARC compare to their engagement in the ELN? One important difference is that, while the FARC took well over a decade to admit women and acknowledge them as equal members, the ELN had female cadres from the beginning. An account of the ELN's history written by one of its leaders notes that one woman was among the organization's original membership: Paula González, also known as "La Mona Mariela." Despite the fact that she was the lone female among the founding group, the organization quickly began to place an emphasis on expanding the diversity of its ranks in terms of gender and social class.[36] However, one hindrance to the group's diversification plan was that over time the ELN evolved into a more decentralized leadership pattern than the FARC displayed. Human Rights Watch notes that field commanders in the ELN had more autonomy compared to other armed groups in Colombia.[37] This autonomy potentially affected the recruitment and treatment of women throughout the ranks.

Officially, the ELN's "code of war" sets sixteen as the minimum age for participation in active combat. Yet interviews with demobilized ELN cadres identify women who joined the organization as young as twelve or thirteen and other women who claimed to have engaged in combat as young as thirteen or fourteen years of age.[38] Interviews by Christiane

Lelièvre Aussel and coauthors also suggest that female membership was higher in urban areas where the ELN was active.[39]

The experiences of women within the ELN likewise varied significantly. Some women worked mostly in gender-stereotyped tasks, as in the FARC, though, unlike the FARC, they were not satisfied with this arrangement and felt that active gender discrimination held them back. Some women reported that their male comrades actively excluded them from political discussions and planning sessions, and there was a sense of frustration that masculine values like strength and bravado were more prized within the group.[40] The ELN has publicly acknowledged some of these complaints. In a 2017 interview a spokeswoman for the ELN admitted that patriarchy "has created some difficulties for women" within the organization, but she emphasized that gender inequality was a comprehensive social problem that the ELN was working to overcome.[41]

The ELN has also tried to position itself as more progressive than the FARC on the subject of reproductive choice. While still discouraged, the ELN has reportedly been more willing to tolerate pregnancies than the FARC.[42] According to an ELN spokeswoman:

> On the topic of motherhood, the organization tries to deal with it to the best of our abilities . . . there are cadres who decide to become mothers outside of the ranks and other cadres who prefer to stay in the ranks and look for ways to be closer to their children. . . . These are the conditions that war creates, but that's not to say *guerrilleras* can't become mothers or that we have to give away our sons and daughters, as some claim.[43]

These statements should be regarded with caution, as there have been reports of forced abortion within the ELN and some female cadres claim they were abandoned by the group after becoming pregnant.[44] Nevertheless, this discourse is noteworthy to the extent that it suggests an attempt by the ELN to distance itself from the accusations of abuse leveled against the FARC as well as from its own history of gender inequality.

Finally, of importance is the position of women within the ELN leadership. We know the personal stories of some individual ELN female leaders, though their biographies are often tinged with rumor and speculation. Comandante Paula (also known as "La Perla Negra") is celebrated as one of the most important women in the history of the ELN and the only woman to be promoted to the organization's national directorate. Paula spent fifty years in the organization, from the age of fifteen until her death at age sixty-five in January 2018. In her final years she was a key member of the ELN's peace negotiating team.[45] Paula allegedly helped found Frente Urbano Resistencia Yariguís or FURY, a particularly active front of the ELN responsible for assassinations and attacks on oil companies. An investigative report by the Colombian newspaper *El Tiempo* alleges that she escaped from jail twice, negotiated territorial disputes with the FARC, and commanded as many as 260 insurgents.[46]

While Paula was the only woman to reach the highest ranks of the ELN, there are other stories of women in leadership roles. La Mona Mariela, the ELN's sole original female member, took part in various armed attacks and supposedly commanded seventy men before disappearing from history.[47] Likewise, "Dora Margarita" features prominently in Patricia Lara's 2000 book on women in armed groups. Dora Margarita is portrayed as an ELN cadre who was appointed as a liaison to the FARC in 1982. She spoke disparagingly of her time with the FARC, particularly their treatment of women. Sometime later she was forced to leave the country and became disillusioned with the ELN. Eventually she shifted her allegiance to M-19 but similarly found that movement unsatisfying. While some scholars appear to have taken Dora Margarita's story at face value,[48] Lara acknowledges that she is in fact a composite character pieced together from multiple narratives.[49] Therefore it is difficult to extrapolate from her story to the women in the ELN in general, although her tale of disillusionment and defection from one armed group to another does ring true to the experience of some women in Colombia.

Pathways to Mobilization

Existing research suggests multiple factors drive women to join Colombia's militant groups. Since the start of the Havana peace talks a number of Farianas have posted their personal stories of mobilization to the Mujer Fariana website and blog. While these *testimonios* are somewhat performative and at times the product of unreliable narrators, it is nonetheless significant that these firsthand accounts echo many of the mobilization themes present in studies of the FARC and other leftist groups in Colombia.[50] For instance, some of the women whose personal stories appear on the site indicate that they either did not know or did not care about the ideology of the FARC before enlisting.[51] This is consistent with research that finds that only 28 percent of female defectors from Colombian armed groups from 2002 to 2004 said they had joined for political or ideological reasons.[52] At the same time, many Farianas assert that they experienced poverty and limited educational opportunities outside the group.[53] This makes sense given the FARC's history of recruiting among the peasantry as well as research indicating that peasant women in Colombia find their lives "hopeless" and are motivated to join an armed group by a lack of opportunity elsewhere.[54]

Fariana narratives also emphasize what most would consider human security concerns—in particular, violence within their communities and families. Many women had experienced violence at the hands of paramilitary groups or state security forces, including raids, looting, disappearances, and displacement.[55] Their stories appear credible, as the timing of many of their stories coincides with a period of organized violence by the state and paramilitary groups against peasants who were believed to be FARC supporters.[56] However, many of these women also experienced violence *within their families*. Academic studies and human rights reports indicate that many women who join armed groups—especially young women—experience some form of domestic violence prior to enlisting.[57] Herrera and Porch estimate that half of all demobilized women in their study had experienced abuse at home; Maria Fernández Luz Londoño and Fernanda Valdivieso Yoana Nieto show that women are twice as likely as men to identify problems in the home as a factor in their decision to join an armed group.[58]

Though "machismo" and an overall climate of gender inequality are often blamed for this pervasive violence, these factors alone do not offer a fully satisfying explanation. A compounding factor in this case may be that many young women who experience domestic violence also are not living with one or either of their parents at the time. Young women interviewed by Londoño and Nieto indicate they were being raised by grandparents or other members of an extended family when they were abused.[59] In a testimonial on the FARC's women's blog, Fariana "Lizeth" describes abuse at the hands of a stepfather.[60] Taken together, these stories suggest that the disruption of poor and rural families—due to mortality, violence, or economic necessity—make young women more susceptible to abuse and more likely to leave abusive homes.

The accessibility of insurgent groups like the FARC enables women to regain a sense of agency and offers a kind of alternative family. Londoño and Nieto highlight that this is also a gendered consideration, as young women and girls are more likely to view themselves as needing a group for protection, compared to young men who may feel more comfortable going it alone.[61] Within territories it controlled, the FARC enforced rules of conduct that outlawed domestic violence, unapproved divorce, and infidelity. Those who violated these rules could be punished through public humiliation, violence, and even death. While such rules were enforced against offenders of either sex, they were generally viewed by women as a positive development.[62] These policies make the FARC seem like a safe haven for those who experience abuse at home.

Once women joined armed groups they frequently moved *between* them. Though the story of Dora Margarita cited above is apocryphal, studies of demobilized women note that they do sometimes move between organizations. Indeed, between the mid-1970s and the early 1990s there was no shortage of options for them. The public emergence of M-19 in 1974 drew some women away from other armed groups. Women who left the ELN to join M-19 cited the charisma of its leadership as well as their disillusionment with other Colombian leftists as factors in their decision making.[63] M-19 in particular took aim at other organizations, portraying the ELN, the FARC, and other groups as backward or myopic in their aims.[64] They identify women as one of the many oppressed populations they sought to empower, and their messages resonated with a female population that was, at that time, excluded from the FARC and discriminated against within the ELN.[65] Women were also approximately one-sixth of the ELN faction that broke away in 1991 to become the Corriente de Renovación Socialista (Socialist Renewal Group, or CRS).[66] The FARC and the ELN reacted to this exodus with efforts to be more gender-inclusive, attempting to outbid their competition and signal their resolve in order to gain an advantage.[67] The competition to appeal to women doubled as a competition to establish legitimacy and bolster the groups' strength.

Women's Engagement in the Peace Process

Among the cases covered in this book, Colombia is the only context in which we can examine the role that female combatants play in peace negotiations. Colombia's peace process is effectively a tale of two processes—an initial phase during the late 1980s and 1990s, during which nine groups (including M-19 and the CRS) reached accords with the government, and a second phase that includes the recent peace negotiations with the FARC and ongoing efforts with the ELN. The temporal distinction is important because the engagement of women at each phase differed dramatically.

The initial phase was largely characterized by a lack of inclusion of women. In spite of the overall presence of women within those groups at their foundings, only one signatory from all the peace agreements that were signed from 1990 to 1994 was female. Even exploratory peace efforts with the FARC and the ELN at this time had few, if any, women in visible roles.[68] It is therefore unsurprising that the DDR processes that followed these negotiations were blind to issues of gender. Women who disarmed during this time were frequently left off official rosters, reports referred to ex-combatants using masculine pronouns, and demobilized women were underrepresented in leadership positions at regional directorates for DDR.[69] Even when a woman became the national director overseeing demobilization in 1998—Gloria Quiceno Vélez, an ex-combatant with M-19—her tenure was characterized by an inattention to gender issues.[70]

Both domestic and international factors explain the radical shift between these early agreements and more recent peace efforts. At the international level, attention from women's groups and the passage of UN Security Council Resolution 1325 in 2000, which called on states to include women in "mechanisms for the prevention, management, and resolution of conflict," created new imperatives for incorporating women.[71] Domestically, women's peace groups that had emerged during the 1980s consolidated and gained influence in the 1990s.[72] The FARC faced pressure from these groups and from María Emma Mejía Vélez—one of the government's principal negotiators under President Andrés Pastrana—to bring women to the peace table.

Women had also gained influence in the ELN and the FARC over the years, in terms of both rank and public recognition. Comandante Paula, in addition to being the only woman to reach the highest level of ELN leadership, gained notoriety for her career with the ELN. She leveraged that increase in stature into an important role in the peace process before her death in 2018. In the FARC, two women in particular elevated their profiles in public-facing roles. Victoria Sandino Palmera, a FARC commander, joined the FARC negotiating team in 2013 and became the first woman to act as the group's spokesperson on the peace process. During the peace talks she amplified her voice by taking to social media, acquiring thousands of Twitter followers. Tanja Nijmeijer (also known as "Alexandra Nariño") acquired international notoriety as a Dutch citizen who joined the FARC in the early 2000s and subsequently took part in a number of attacks on the Colombian government. She was the subject of multiple documentaries, biographies, and news stories—including the publication of extracts from her private diary in 2007. Her appointment to the FARC's negotiating team in 2012 was regarded by some as a move to capitalize on her notoriety.[73] Since the conclusion of the Havana peace talks in 2016, the ELN has appointed more women to the role of spokesperson for the organization, yet another example of one armed group adopting the successful tactics of another.[74]

Over the years of negotiations in Havana between the government and the FARC, a number of Farianas took part in the talks. Many were involved in the work of the Gender Subcommission, the body assigned with ensuring that gender concerns were adequately addressed in all substantive aspects of the accords. This body, historic in the context of global peace agreements, also engaged women who represented the government, the Colombian military, and various third parties.[75] Women who participated on behalf of the FARC were selected with a variety of criteria in mind, including seniority, communication ability, whether they spoke multiple languages, and whether they had previously interacted with civil society organizations.[76]

In interviews following the talks, women from the government delegation complimented their FARC counterparts, expressing surprise and admiration regarding their discipline and preparation.[77] Among the achievements of the commission were that the final peace accords included provisions that prioritize female heads-of-household in rural development programs, that create programs aimed at promoting women's leadership and political participation, and that guarantee the inclusion of women in the citizen-oversight organizations responsible for implementing the accords.[78] While it is unclear what specific gender-related provisions may be included in a future agreement with the ELN, María Consuelo Tapias—one of the female delegates to the peace talks—has said in interviews that she comes to the table bringing both her identity as a woman and her identity as an ELN member. She believes gender issues are important to address in all aspects of the negotiation agenda.[79]

Conclusions

An examination of gender in the FARC, the ELN, and the broader context of the Colombian conflict illuminates a few key themes. First is the process of organizational learning that took place among the groups as they incorporated women and addressed gender issues in their ideologies. The FARC, which initially sidelined women, changed its policies after the ELN, M-19, and others incorporated women into their ranks and mainstreamed gender issues into their broader agendas. This change, occurring in the 1980s, also happened at a time when the field of leftist armed groups in Colombia was crowded and competitive. Later the FARC was once again pressured—this time by both domestic and international actors—to increase the visibility of women as it entered peace negotiations. Today the ELN seems to be emulating the FARC with the appointment of female negotiators and pledges to mainstream gender issues in a possible future peace accord.

This interplay among guerrilla organizations is best understood as an outbidding process. Colombia demonstrates the necessary characteristics for outbidding: multiple groups with similar ideologies existing in the same place and time and appealing to demographically similar constituencies.[80] Through this lens the promotion and inclusion of women and gender issues represent a series of signals meant to cultivate legitimacy and convey a commitment to leftist ideals. Our analysis therefore arrives at three primary conclusions:

- Enlistment in an armed rebel group in Colombia was a means to escape poverty, government repression, or a dysfunctional home life, particularly for women who joined the FARC. Earlier studies suggest that, across armed groups, women did not have strong ideological commitments prior to enlisting.
- An environment of outbidding created options for women, giving them the ability to move between armed groups that actively courted their support.
- The expansion of women's roles and influence in the FARC and the ELN—especially in the respective peace processes with the Colombian government—has been driven by both domestic and international factors.

The full impact of women's participation in Colombian conflicts is still coming into focus. By engaging in peace negotiations, women in the FARC and the ELN attained a level of visibility and influence that they could not normally reach through formal internal leadership structures. Yet, developments since the 2016 peace agreement raise questions about the ability of the Colombian government to effectively reintegrate combatants, particularly women. The peace agreement designated certain sites where FARC guerrillas could participate in programming and job training following disarmament, though by mid-2018 more than half of the FARC's cadres had left those sites and faced an uncertain future.[81]

The UN has expressed concern that Colombia lacks the resources to effectively reintegrate disarmed combatants into society. Acts of violence against FARC members, including political candidates participating in the democratic process, reinforce these concerns.[82] The economic and political crisis in Venezuela creates new challenges, with the ELN and breakaway EPL factions both active and reportedly recruiting FARC dissidents there.[83] In addition to the stigma attached to being a former guerrilla, ex-Farianas bear the burden of past abortions or being perceived as promiscuous. Many would like to start families, and some are looking to reunite with families they left behind. However, the lack of resources for reintegration, the chilly climate toward ex-guerrillas, and the patriarchal attitudes that prevail in Colombia call into question whether they will be able to retain the relationships they formed during conflict or put their career training to use in the future.[84] These obstacles are similar to ones faced by women in other Colombian rebel groups that disarmed during the 1990s and early 2000s. If their concerns are not adequately addressed, they will almost certainly reappear after any future peace accord with the ELN.

Notes

Epigraph: Rosemberg Pabón, *Así Nos Tomamos la Embajada* (This is how we took the embassy) (Madrid: Planeta, 1984), 60–61, as quoted in Rojas Pacheco and Maria Herminia, "Las Mujeres en los Procesos de Paz en Colombia" (Women in the Colombian peace processes), *Caliban: Revista Cubana de Pensamiento e Historia*, 2014, accessed March 7, 2018, http://www.revistacaliban.cu/articulo.php?numero=19&article_id=191.

1. Steven Pinker and Juan Manuel Santos, "Colombia's Milestone in World Peace," *New York Times*, January 20, 2018, https://www.nytimes.com/2016/08/26/opinion/colombias-milestone-in-world-peace.html.

2. UN Women, "Joint Statement by Phumzile Mlambo-Ngcuka and Zainab Hawa Bangura on the Historic Commitment by the Government of Colombia and FARC-EP at the Havana Peace Talks Table," news release, July 26, 2016, http://www.unwomen.org/en/news/stories/2016/7/joint-statement-by-phumzile-mlambo-ngcuka-and-zainab-hawa-bangura.

3. The UN defines gender mainstreaming as "the process of assessing the implications for men and women of any planned action, including legislation, policies or programmes, in all areas and at all levels," UN General Assembly, Report A/52/3, "Report of the Economic and Social Council 1997," September 18, 1997, 27–38, http://undocs.org/A/52/3.

4. Pablo Castillo Diaz and Simon Tordjman, *Women's Participation in Peace Negotiations: Connections between Presence and Influence*, 2nd ed. (New York: UN

Women, 2012), http://reliefweb.int/sites/reliefweb.int/files/resources/03A WomenPeaceNeg.pdf.

5. Sarah Zukerman Daly, *Organized Violence after Civil War: The Geography of Recruitment in Latin America* (Cambridge: Cambridge University Press, 2016); Jacqueline O'Neill, "Are Women the Key to Peace in Colombia?" *Foreign Policy*, April 21, 2015, https://foreignpolicy.com/2015/04/20/are-women-the-key-to -peace-in-colombia-farc-talks/.

6. This is down from an estimated peak of four thousand members in the year 2000. Pablo Medina Uribe, "Beyond the FARC: Colombia's Other Illegal Armed Groups Explained," *AS/COA*, June 1, 2016, http://www.as-coa.org/articles/beyond -farc-colombias-other-illegal-armed-groups-explained; "National Liberation Army (Colombia)," Mapping Militant Organizations, accessed August 30, 2018, http://web.stanford.edu/group/mappingmilitants/cgi-bin/groups/view/87#size; "Profiles: Colombia's Armed Groups," *BBC News*, August 29, 2013, http://www .bbc.com/news/world-latin-america-11400950.

7. Jamille Bigio, Rachel Vogelstein, and Anne Connell, "Women's Participation in Peace Processes: Colombia," *Council on Foreign Relations* blog, December 15, 2017, https://www.cfr.org/blog/womens-participation-peace-processes-colombia.

8. The EPL officially disbanded in 1991, although a splinter group of seventy to one hundred fighters continued to engage the government using the EPL name. The government refers to this as a "dissident faction." No armed attacks have been attributed to the group since its leader, Víctor Ramón Navarro, known as "Megateo," was killed by the government in 2015. The current status and membership of the organization is unclear. "Popular Liberation Army," Mapping Militant Organizations, August 29, 2015, http://web.stanford.edu/group/mappingmili tants/cgi-bin/groups/view/119; Uribe, "Beyond the FARC."

9. Daly, *Organized Violence after Civil War*; "Popular Liberation Army"; Charles W. Bergquist, Ricardo Peñaranda, and G. Gonzalo Sánchez, *Violence in Colombia, 1990–2000: Waging War and Negotiating Peace* (Wilmington, DE: Scholarly Resources, 2001).

10. Laura Linero and Carlos Morales, "Las Cifras de los 10 Años de Desmovilizaciones" (Figures from ten years of demobilizations), *El Tiempo*, accessed August 30, 2018, http://www.eltiempo.com/Multimedia/especiales/desmoviliza dos/ARCHIVO/ARCHIVO-12224321-0.pdf.

11. This and other documents referenced in this section were obtained from the archives of the Centro de Documentación de los Movimientos Armados (CeDeMA).

12. "Programa Agrario de los Guerrilleros" (Agrarian program of the guerrillas), CeDeMA, accessed August 30, 2018, http://www.cedema.org/ver.php?id=4021.

13. Francisco Gutiérrez Sanín and Francy Carranza Franco, "Organizing Women for Combat: The Experience of the FARC in the Colombian War," *Journal of Agrarian Change* 17, no. 4 (2017): 770–78, doi:10.1111/joac.12238.

14. "Declaración Politica de la Segunda Conferencia Guerrillera del Bloque Sur" (Political declaration of the second guerrilla conference of the southern bloc), CeDeMA, accessed August 30, 2018, http://www.cedema.org/ver.php?id=4415.

15. Alfredo Molano, "The Evolution of the FARC: A Guerrilla Group's Long History," *NACLA Report on the Americas* 34, no. 2 (2000): 23–31, doi:10.1080/10 714839.2000.11722627.

16. Manuel Marulanda Vélez, *Resistencia De Un Pueblo En Armas* (Resistance of a people in arms) (Bogota: Ocean Sur, 2015); Sanín and Franco, "Organizing Women for Combat."

17. Julia Eriksson, "Women in Leadership and Sexual Violence—A Case Study of the Role of Women in FARC," undergraduate thesis, Uppsala University, 2017, http://urn.kb.se/resolve?urn=urn%3Anbn%3Ase%3Auu%3Adiva-319493; Natalia Herrera and Douglas Porch, "'Like Going to a Fiesta'—The Role of Female Fighters in Colombia's FARC-EP," *Small Wars and Insurgencies* 19, no. 4 (2008): 609–34, doi:10.1080/09592310802462547.

18. ELN, "Manifiesto de Simacota," CeDeMA, January 7, 1965, http://www .cedema.org/ver.php?id=3703.

19. Claire Felter and Danielle Renwick, "Colombia's Civil Conflict," *Council on Foreign Relations*, January 11, 2017, https://www.cfr.org/backgrounder /colombias-civil-conflict.

20. Roberto Sancho Larrañaga, *Guerrilla y Terrorismo en Colombia y España: ELN y ETA* (Guerrilla warfare and terrorism in Colombia and Spain: The ELN and ETA) (Bucaramanga, Colombia: Editorial U. Autónoma Bucaramanga, 2003); Uribe, "Beyond the FARC."

21. Sancho Larrañaga, *Guerilla y Terrorismo*, 181–83.

22. Examples of this are discussed later. Many of the joint communiqués and open letters exchanged among various groups and published over the years are also archived on the CeDeMA website.

23. Sanín and Franco, "Organizing Women for Combat."

24. Human Rights Watch, *"You'll Learn Not to Cry": Child Combatants in Colombia* (New York: Human Rights Watch, 2003), 58–59, https://www.hrw.org /reports/2003/colombia0903/colombia0903.pdf.

25. "Guerrilla Women Have the Right to Know Where Their Children Are," *FARC-EP International*, April 7, 2017, http://farc-epeace.org/peace-process/news /item/1153-guerrilla-women-have-the-right-to-know-where-their-children-are .html.

26. "Guerrilla Women Have the Right."

27. "Guerrilla Women Have the Right."

28. Alexandra Welsh, "Women of the Jungle: Guerrilleras on the Front Lines of the FARC-EP," *Glendon Journal of International Studies* 8, nos. 1–2 (2015): 1–14, https://gjis.journals.yorku.ca/index.php/gjis/article/view/39078; Herrera and Porch, "Like Going to a Fiesta."

29. Garry M. Leech, *The FARC: The Longest Insurgency* (London: Zed, 2012).

30. Herrera and Porch, "Like Going to a Fiesta"; Welsh, "Women of the Jungle."

31. Sanín and Franco, "Organizing Women for Combat."

32. Herrera and Porch, "Like Going to a Fiesta"; Human Rights Watch, "*You'll Learn Not to Cry.*"

33. Herrera and Porch, "Like Going to a Fiesta," 627.

34. Leech, *Longest Insurgency*; Welsh, "Women of the Jungle"; Sanín and Franco, "Organizing Women for Combat."

35. Herrera and Porch, "Like Going to a Fiesta."

36. Milton Hernández, *Rojo y Negro: Historia del ELN* (Red and black: History of the ELN) (Tafalla, Spain: Editorial Txalaparta, 2006), 120.

37. Human Rights Watch, "*You'll Learn Not to Cry,*" 25.

38. Human Rights Watch, "*You'll Learn Not to Cry*"; Christiane Lelièvre Aussel, Graciliana Echavarría, and Isabel Ortiz Pérez, *Haciendo Memoria y Dejando Rastros: Encuentros con Mujeres Excombatientes del Nororiente de Colombia* (Making memories and leaving traces: Encounters with female veterans of northeast Colombia) (Bogota: Fundación Mujer y Futuro, 2004), http://www.bdigital.unal.edu.co/45755/1/9583369004.pdf.

39. Lelièvre Aussel et al., *Haciendo Memoria y Dejando Rastros*, 72.

40. Lelièvre Aussel et al., *Haciendo Memoria y Dejando Rastros*, 97–98.

41. "Mujeres del ELN Colombiano: 'La Paz Para Nosotras Es Diversidad, Por Lo Que la Participación Es Fundamental'" (Women of the Colombian ELN: "Peace for us is diversity, so participation is fundamental"), *Resumen Latinoamericano*, January 11, 2017, http://www.resumenlatinoamericano.org/2017/01/12/mujeres-del-eln-colombiano-la-paz-para-nosotras-es-diversidad-por-lo-que-la-participacion-es-fundamental/.

42. Human Rights Watch, "*You'll Learn Not to Cry,*" 59.

43. "Mujeres del ELN Colombiano."

44. Human Rights Watch, "*You'll Learn Not to Cry*"; Sara Reardon, "Colombia: After the Violence," *Nature News*, May 2, 2018, https://www.nature.com/immersive/d41586-018-04976-7/index.html.

45. "Homenaje a la Comandante Paula" (Tribute to comandante Paula), YouTube video, 5:12, posted by ELN Paz, January 18, 2018, https://www.youtube.com/watch?v=GaIXI92LdoM.

46. "La Historia de la Jefa del ELN Que Se Apareció en Caracas" (The story of the ELN leader who appeared in Caracas), *El Tiempo*, April 9, 2016, http://www.eltiempo.com/archivo/documento/CMS-16559600.

47. As recently as early 2018 there were claims that La Mona Mariela was still alive and secretly living somewhere in Colombia. Julian Gabriel Parra-De Moya, "En Busca de la Mona Mariela: el Mito Guerrillero del ELN" (In search of Mona Mariela: The mythical ELN guerrilla), *Las2orillas*, January 17, 2018, https://www.las2orillas.co/en-busca-de-la-mona-mariela-el-mito-gu errillero-del-eln/.

48. See, for example, Herrera and Porch, "Like Going to a Fiesta."

49. Patricia Lara Salive, *La Mujeres en la Guerra* (Women in war) (Bogota: Planeta Colombiana, 2000), 19.

50. See, for example, Cherilyn Elston, *Women's Writing in Colombia: An Alternative History* (Cham, Switzerland: Palgrave Macmillan, 2016). See also Khagendra Acharya and Orla T. Muldoon, "Why 'I' Became a Combatant: A Study of Memoirs Written by Nepali Maoist Combatants," *Terrorism and Political Violence* 29, no. 6 (2015): 1006–25, doi:10.1080/09546553.2015.1105797; and Esin Duzel, "Fragile Goddesses: Moral Subjectivity and Militarized Agencies in Female Guerrilla Diaries and Memoirs," *International Feminist Journal of Politics* 20, no. 2 (2018): 137–52, doi:10.1080/14616742.2017.1419823, on the similar and performative roles of narrative among female insurgents in the PKK and the CPN-M in Nepal.

51. Yorleny Duque, "La Violencia Me Hizo Guerrillera" (Violence made me a guerrilla), *Mujer Fariana*, March 18, 2017, http://www.mujerfariana.org/vision/798 -la-violencia-me-hizo-guerrillera.html; "La Crónica de Lizeth, Escrita Por Ella Misma" (The chronicle of Lizeth, written herself), *Mujer Fariana*, November 11, 2013, http://www.mujerfariana.org/vision/94-la-cronica-de-lizeth-escrita-por -ella-misma.html.

52. This analysis draws on a sample of women who defected from the FARC (57 percent), various leftist groups, including the ELN (22 percent), and paramilitary organizations, including the AUC (Maria Fernández Luz Londoño and Fernanda Valdivieso Yoana Nieto, *Mujeres No Contadas: Procesos de Desmovilización y Retorno a La Vida Civil de Mujeres Excombatientes En Colombia, 1990–2003* (Uncounted women: Processes of demobilization and return to civilian life for ex-combatant women in Colombia, 1990–2003) (Medellín, Colombia: Instituto de Estudios Regionales, Universidad de Antioquia, 2007), 114–16.

53. "La Crónica de Lizeth"; Duque, "La Violencia Me Hizo Guerrillera"; "Entrevista de Farianas a Maryeli Ospina Guerrillera de Las FARC-EP" (Interview by Fariana of Maryeli Ospina, FARC guerrilla), *Mujer Fariana*, August 23, 2016, http://www.mujerfariana.org/vision/678-entrevista-de-farianas-a-maryeli -ospina-guerrillera-de-las-farc-ep.html; Gonzalo Sánchez et al., *Mujeres y Guerra. Víctimas y Resistentes En El Caribe Colombiano* (Women and war. Victims and resisters in Colombia's Caribbean region) (Bogota: Centro de Memoria Historica, 2014), http://www.centrodememoriahistorica.gov.co/informes/informes-2011 /mujeres-y-guerra.

54. Margaret Gonzalez-Perez, "Guerrilleras in Latin America: Domestic and International Roles," *Journal of Peace Research* 43, no. 3 (2006): 313–29, doi:10.1177 /0022343306063934; Margaret Gonzalez-Perez, *Women and Terrorism: Female Activity in Domestic and International Terror Groups* (London: Routledge, 2008); Herrera and Porch, "Like Going to a Fiesta."

55. Duque, "La Violencia Me Hizo Guerrillera"; "La Crónica de Lizeth"; "Entrevista de Farianas"; Daniela Sánchez, "Esta Es Mi Historia" (This is my story), *Mujer Fariana*, March 21, 2017, http://www.mujerfariana.org/vision/804-esta-es -mi-historia.html.

56. Welsh, "Women of the Jungle."

57. Saridalia Giraldo, "Demobilized Women Combatants: Lessons from Colombia," paper presented at the Twenty-Second Annual Graduate Student Research Conference, UCLA Center for the Study of Women, Los Angeles, February 3, 2012, https://escholarship.org/uc/item/08z6h9qk#page-7; Herrera and Porch, "Like Going to a Fiesta"; Human Rights Watch, *"You'll Learn to Not Cry"*; Londoño and Nieto, *Mujeres No Contadas*.

58. Herrera and Porch, "Like Going to a Fiesta"; Londoño and Nieto, *Mujeres No Contadas*, 116.

59. Londoño and Nieto, *Mujeres No Contadas*, 224.

60. "Entrevista de Farianas."

61. Londoño and Nieto, *Mujeres No Contadas*, 223.

62. Maria Clemencia Ramirez, Maria Luisa Moreno R., and Camila Medina A., *El Placer: Mujeres, Coca, y Guerra En El Bajo Putumayo* (El Placer: Women, cocaine, and war in Bajo Putumayo) (Bogota: Centro de Memoria Historica, 2012), accessed August 30, 2018, http://centrodememoriahistorica.gov.co/descargas /informes2012/el_placer.pdf.

63. Lelièvre Aussel et al., *Haciendo Memoria y Dejando Rastros*, 36–37, 67.

64. Lelièvre Aussel et al., *Haciendo Memoria y Dejando Rastros*, 38.

65. "Bolívar, Tu Espada Vuelve a La Lucha" (Bolivar, your sword returns to the fight), CeDeMA, January 17, 1974, http://cedema.org/ver.php?id=3718.

66. Virginia Bouvier, *UN Women Background Paper: Gender and the Role of Women in Colombia's Peace Process* (New York: US Institute for Peace, 2016), 4, https://www.usip.org/sites/default/files/Gender-and-the-Role-of-Women-in -Colombia-s-Peace-Process-English.pdf.

67. Andrew H. Kydd and Barbara F. Walter, "The Strategies of Terrorism," *International Security* 31, no. 1 (2006): 49–80, doi:10.1162/isec.2006.31.1.49.

68. Bouvier, *UN Women Background Paper*, 17.

69. Bouvier, *UN Women Background Paper*; Londoño and Nieto, *Mujeres No Contada*, 88–89.

70. Londoño and Nieto, *Mujeres No Contada*, 88.

71. UN Security Council, Resolution 1325, October 31, 2000, http://daccess -ods.un.org/access.nsf/Get?Open&DS=S/RES/1325(2000)&Lang=E.

72. Gonzalo Sánchez et al., *Mujeres y Guerra*.

73. Elyssa Pachico, "Dutch FARC Guerrilla Arrives in Cuba (and Sings about It)," *InSight Crime*, October 6, 2017, https://www.insightcrime.org/news/analysis /dutch-guerrilla-farc-cuba-sings/.

74. "Mujeres del ELN Colombiano."

75. "Joint Statement by Phumzile Mlambo-Ngcuka and Zainab Hawa Bangura."

76. July Samira Fajardo Farfan and Juliana Suescún, *Vivencias, Aportes y Reconocimiento: Las Mujeres En El Proceso De Paz En La Habana* (Experiences, contributions, and recognition: Women in the peace process in Havana) (Bogota: UN Women, 2017), 23, http://colombia.unwomen.org/es/biblioteca/publicaciones/2017/05/mujeres-en-la-habana.

77. Fajardo Farfan and Suescún, *Vivencias, Aportes*, 90.

78. See, among others, provisions 1.1.2–3, 2.2.5, 2.3.5, and 2.3.7 of the final peace agreement: Colombia, Office of the High Commissioner for Peace, *Final Peace Agreement*, November 24, 2016, http://www.altocomisionadoparalapaz.gov.co/Prensa/Documentoscompartidos/Colombian-Peace-Agreement-English-Translation.pdf.

79. "La Mujer y Su Participación En Los Diálogos Del ELN y El Gobierno Colombiano" (Women and their participation in the dialogues between the ELN and the Colombian government), *Trochando Sin Fronteras*, February 8, 2017, https://trochandosinfronteras.info/la-mujer-y-su-participacion-en-los-dialogos-del-eln-y-el-gobierno-colombiano/.

80. Kydd and Walter, "Strategies of Terrorism."

81. Reardon, "Colombia."

82. Edith M. Lederer, "UN Official: Reintegrating Colombia Rebels Is Not Going Well," *Chicago Tribune*, October 21, 2017, http://webcache.googleusercontent.com/search?q=cache:jSjK1mraf2EJ:www.chicagotribune.com/sns-bc-un—united-nations-colombia-20171020-story.html; Reardon, "Colombia."

83. While both groups have denied responsibility for some of the most vicious attacks, ELN and EPL holdouts (also known as "Los Pelusos") are engaged in armed struggle along the border. FARC dissidents, also active in the area, are believed to have joined both groups. Catatumbo is strategically important for the survival of armed organizations; it is well-suited for the cultivation and transport of coca, and its proximity to the border has allowed for a thriving black market in the transportation of gasoline. Recent attacks include shoot-outs, the seizure of territory, and the murder of Venezuelan soldiers. With their attention focused elsewhere, analysts have accused Venezuela of turning a blind eye to armed groups that carry out activities on their side of the border. For their part, the ELN and the Pelusos have both reached out to Venezuelan citizens, offering school supplies, Christmas gifts, and other provisions to cultivate goodwill among the struggling population. Though the gender balance of the Pelusos is not definitively known, one recent estimate suggests they are roughly three hundred strong and continually recruiting. See Ronna Rísquez and Victoria Dittmar, "ELN and EPL Conflict Intensifies at Colombia-Venezuela Border," *Insight Crime*, August 2, 2018, https://www.insightcrime.org/news/brief/eln-epl-conflict-intensifies-colombia-venezuela-border/; Anadolu Agency, "Las Cinco Denuncias Sobre Presencia del

ELN en Venezuela" (Five complaints about the ELN presence in Venezuela), *El Espectador*, April 26, 2018, https://www.elespectador.com/noticias/el-mundo/las -cinco-denuncias-sobre-presencia-del-eln-en-venezuela-articulo-752300; "¿Por Qué Es la Guerra Entre el ELN y el EPL Que Deja Muertos y Desplazados en el Catatumbo?" (Why is the war between ELN and EPL leaving dead and displaced people in Catatumbo?) *El Espectador*, April 23, 2018, https://www.elespectador .com/noticias/nacional/por-que-es-la-guerra-entre-el-eln-y-el-epl-que-deja -muertos-y-desplazados-en-el-catatumbo-video-751594; Adriaan Alsema, "EPL/ Los Pelusos," *Colombia Reports,* March 26, 2017, https://colombiareports.com /epl-pelusos/.

84. Sruthi Gottipati, "Colombia's Female FARC Fighters Wage a New War, for Gender Parity," *IRIN*, March 8, 2017, https://www.irinnews.org/feature/2017 /09/07/colombia-s-female-farc-fighters-wage-new-war-gender-parity; Emily Wright, "The End of FARC's Fifty-Year Pregnancy Ban Leads to a Baby Boom," *Public Radio International,* July 20, 2017, https://www.pri.org/stories/2017–07–20 /end-farcs-50-year-pregnancy-ban-leads-baby-boom.

Conclusions and Implications

Women are a fundamental part of the landscape of war. From Colombia to Syria, women's participation as combatants represents an important feature of conflict. We draw lessons from our analyses and look beyond these cases to identify commonalities with other contemporary nonstate armed groups that recruit women. We also examine the implications of our research for policies aimed at mitigating recruitment into armed groups as well as encouraging participation in DDR programs.

Broadly, our findings indicate that:

- There is no single profile of a female combatant.
- Motivations for joining nonstate armed groups and participating in violence vary among individual women, just as they do among individual men.
- Women serve in a broad range of roles within many contemporary nonstate armed groups, including as fighters.
- The degree to which nonstate armed groups explicitly appeal to women, especially in recruitment, is an outgrowth of women's participation in the group itself.
- Women willingly participate in nonstate armed groups even when those groups are hostile to or victimize women.
- Female combatants face distinct challenges that need to be addressed in peace accords and in DDR programs.

Lessons Learned

In spite of the differences between the nonstate armed groups examined in this book, many similarities are worth nothing. These similarities can help inform policies to address some of the specific challenges posed by the involvement of female combatants in civil wars.

There is no single profile of a female fighter. Women of different ages, religions, ethnicities, social backgrounds, marital status, and a host of other characteristics participate in civil wars. Female fighters are a truly global phenomenon. However, individual armed factions may appeal to certain groups or have particular policies with regard to the women they recruit. Separatist rebel groups in Ukraine have a greater number of women in their thirties and even forties than their pro-government counterparts. Women in Ukrainian separatist groups are also more likely to be fighting in the region they call home. On the other hand, there is sometimes variation even within a single group; while the early PKK recruited large numbers of poorly educated rural women, it also drew educated recruits from universities in urban areas.

The motivations of individual women are varied, and those differences in motivation matter. In all the groups we examined, there were women who deeply believed in and were motivated by the cause or platform of the group. Cross-national research covering groups over the past four decades has found that a rebel group's political ideology plays a central role in women's participation: Marxist or leftist-oriented rebel groups have a relatively higher prevalence of female participants; an Islamist ideology has the opposite effect.[1] This finding was mirrored in our analysis of the FARC and the ELN in Colombia and Kurdish armed groups in Syria and Turkey. However, our analyses also identified a range of other motivations for women's participation in nonstate armed groups, including a threat to personal security, proximity to the conflict, a desire for personal autonomy, and close personal connections with others who had taken up arms.

Women often serve in a range of roles, including combat roles, within nonstate armed groups. Some women have even taken on leadership roles in armed groups. Indeed, in the case of the PKK in Turkey, women's equality within the organization, including in leadership positions, is a matter of organizational policy. However, the relative balance in women's participation in support versus combat roles varies widely across armed groups.

While women in Ukrainian armed groups appear to be almost universally trained in handling arms (with the possible exception being medics), only limited evidence indicates that they actually participate in combat. Women are more likely to be seen staffing checkpoints and serving in logistical and support roles. In Colombia, women were initially mobilized into the FARC alongside their families; they performed supporting roles, such as maintaining camps and cooking meals. Only later were women accepted as fighters. Unlike other Kurdish armed groups, women play a relatively limited role in the Iraqi Kurdish forces known collectively as the peshmerga.

The degree to which nonstate armed groups directly appeal to women in their recruitment and/or propaganda is largely an outgrowth of women's participation itself. Women have played key roles as recruiters and propagandists—serving as the vehicle for the recruitment of other women. The adoption of a gender rights platform is a product of the engagement and advancement of women within a group like the FARC; that is, it is an internal development rather than a strategic top-down maneuver. The early involvement of women in the PKK—in combination with a leadership that was already ideologically sympathetic to women's participation—meant that when the Turkish crackdown on the Kurdish regions of Turkey in the 1990s politicized many women, the PKK was already well-positioned to recruit them into its armed forces.

Women participate in armed groups even when those groups maintain policies that negatively affect them. Though some groups—including the ELN in Colombia and the PKK in Turkey—feature high-profile female leaders, overall relatively few women are leaders of insurgent groups. Interviews with women in Kurdish armed groups indicate the continued discrimination that women face, even when they have access to power within these groups. The general hostility of armed groups toward women manifests itself in other ways as well. The FARC's policy of forced abortion and contraception is the clearest example of a relatively egalitarian group maintaining policies that directly discriminate against women and limit their ability to make their own decisions. The use of women as suicide bombers—in the PKK and other groups—raises important questions about women's agency within nonstate armed groups.

Women in Salafi-Jihadi Groups

To provide additional evidence and context for these findings, analysis of three additional nonstate armed actors is instructive: ISIS, Boko Haram, and al-Shabaab. These three groups share several key characteristics, including their adherence to a violent Salafi ideology, their ability to hold and control territory, and their extensive reliance on women in support roles.

The Islamic State (ISIS)

The widespread mobilization of women in support of war is perhaps most evident in ISIS. Women and girls from at least twenty-one countries, from France to Russia to Indonesia, have been identified in territory held by ISIS.[2] Estimates indicate that at least 1,780 foreign women joined ISIS, albeit not as combatants.[3] Take tiny Kosovo, in the heart of the Balkans, as one example. A country of less than 2 million people, Kosovo has had more than 300 citizens leave for Iraq or Syria since 2012. Of these, 55 (or about 15 percent) are women or girls.[4] As of July 2018 only 7 Kosovar women had returned, a rate of 12.7 percent, compared to the estimated 45 percent of Kosovar men who returned after joining ISIS abroad. Kosovo in this sense typifies larger trends among ISIS returnees. Research by Joana Cook and Gina Vale concludes that the number of women affiliated with ISIS overall has been "significantly underestimated," while the gender gap in return rates between male and female foreign fighters raises red flags surrounding the fate of "missing" ISIS women.[5]

Some of the most detailed information available on foreign women who joined ISIS comes from a guesthouse registry recovered by the US military in Syria. It indicates that of the 1,132 females who stayed at the guesthouse, 75 percent were already married.[6] While the average age of women at the guesthouse was twenty-nine, female guests ranged in age from eleven to seventy-six; just 20 percent were age twenty-one or younger. This new evidence challenges media accounts of "jihadi brides" lured by the promise of affection from men in the so-called caliphate.[7] But it also confirms that family ties are an important pathway into militant groups. That being said, research on Western women's motivations for joining the group has identified religious ideology and feelings of isolation and disaffection as factors driving their mobilization. Meredith Loken and Anna Zelenz ultimately conclude that Western women join ISIS for largely the same reasons as male recruits.[8]

Women also play key roles in ISIS as recruiters and propagandists.[9] On social media, women have been quick to support the extreme violence that

ISIS carries out and have worked to recruit other women.[10] In *Al Dabiq*, ISIS's glossy English-language magazine, a female writer using the name "Al Muhajjira" published a full-throated defense of ISIS's practice of enslaving women and girls.[11] Another writer claiming to be affiliated with the all-female al-Khansaa brigade published an Arabic-language pamphlet extolling the position of women under the "Islamic State" and decrying the roles played by women elsewhere.[12] While women are actively recruited to the caliphate to serve as wives and mothers, they also serve in other roles and are permitted to work as nurses, doctors, and teachers in a highly gender-segregated environment, though under very specific conditions.[13]

While far fewer women are in active combat positions in ISIS than in other nonstate armed groups, some women have nevertheless served as suicide bombers, snipers, or torturers.[14] The first confirmed report of a female combatant in ISIS was in February 2016, but unconfirmed reports of female ISIS fighters in Syria date back to July 2014.[15] Two all-female ISIS police units, the al-Khansaa Brigade and Umm Al-Rayan, are often seen as quasi-military in nature.[16] More women might have taken on combat roles if they had been allowed to do so; one recruit from the West expressed disappointment in not being allowed to fight for the group despite having a military background.[17] Some analysts suggest that more women may take on combat roles as ISIS evolves following its loss of territory in Iraq and Syria, but this remains disputed.[18]

Boko Haram

Boko Haram, active primarily in northeastern Nigeria and its bordering regions, has also relied extensively on women both on and off the battlefield. The group is perhaps most famous for its forced recruitment of women, including the 2014 mass kidnapping of 276 schoolgirls from Chibok that spawned the #BringBackOurGirls movement.[19] In February 2018, 110 more girls were kidnapped in the town of Dapchi.[20] While specific details about women's roles within Boko Haram remain murky, women and girls have been sold as slaves, forcibly married to fighters, and, over time, emerged as the majority of suicide bombers for the group.[21]

One study of Boko Haram found that at least 56 percent of the group's suicide bombers during the period from April 2011 to June 2017 were female.[22] Jason Warner and Hilary Matfess identify a distinct rise in the use of multiple female suicide bombers in individual attacks, just two months after the Chibok kidnappings.[23] Such attacks are likely to continue. In May 2018 four female suicide bombers conducted an attack that killed at least four people and injured nine others in Maiduguri, Nigeria.[24] Warner and Matfess argue that Boko Haram's female suicide bombers are a reflection of the group's recruitment tactics as well as a female social base that is willing to tolerate and perpetrate such attacks. While female suicide bombers have been used widely by other armed groups—including the PKK; the Al Aqsa Martyrs Brigade (which is associated with Fatah); Hamas; the Liberation Tigers of Tamil Eelam (the LTTE, commonly known as the Tamil Tigers); and various Chechen groups in Russia—Boko Haram's combination of forced recruitment and suicide bombing brings into question women's agency in a way not seen in the cases examined here.[25]

Al-Shabaab

An affiliate of al Qaeda operating in Somalia and Kenya, al-Shabaab's strength was estimated to be between seven and nine thousand fighters in late 2017. There are no authoritative estimates of the number of women associated with the terrorist group, although women's involvement has clearly been essential to its longevity. Family ties have played an important role in recruitment; as with ISIS, women have followed their husbands into al-Shabaab. Another commonality al-Shabaab has with ISIS is that girls and women have been forced into marriages and sexual servitude, irrespective of whether or not they willingly joined the group.

While research on women's participation in al-Shabaab remains limited, economic and familial motivations are cited more frequently than ideological ones. Narratives from women who have escaped the group identify personal issues such as an inability to pay school fees, joblessness, or a search for work abroad as factors in their recruitment.[26] Many women who are trafficked into al-Shabaab against their will are lured with the promise of a paid position as a cook or cleaner.[27] One study suggests that female-headed households in Kenya may be particularly susceptible to the economic incentives offered by al-Shabaab.[28] But research also suggests that recruiters are expanding beyond economically vulnerable women to women studying in institutions of higher learning as well.[29] If the effort proves successful, it would offer further evidence that women's motivations for joining armed movements are as complex and multifaceted as men's.

Not all women involved with al-Shabaab serve in noncombat positions; testimonies from returnees attest to the presence of female fighters.[30] One Kenyan initially left to find work in Somalia on the recommendation of a family member: "When I got to the camp I received religious and weapons training, which involved combat and suicide bombing training. I was a virgin when I arrived. Soon after, I refused to have sex with one of the fighters. When he tried to force himself on me, I fought him off and stabbed him. He died."[31] After this incident she was promoted to commander and placed in charge of the approximately forty women in her camp. This narrative and others suggest that the group provides combat training to some women, although it remains unclear whether it is available to the majority of women in the group. In practice few women have been directly implicated in al-Shabaab attacks. A September 2016 attack on a police station in the Kenyan city of Mombasa that involved three women was attributed to the group, but such attacks are relatively rare.[32] Less than 5 percent of al-Shabaab's suicide bombers have been identified as female. This has led analysts to conclude that the group is bucking the trend among African nonstate armed groups of having more women serving as suicide bombers.[33]

More commonly, women in al-Shabaab serve in support roles: preparing food, collecting firewood, providing medical care, and sheltering or hiding other members. Women outside of Somalia and Kenya have played an active role in financing al-Shabaab,[34] and still others have worked as recruiters.[35] Kenyan women who have participated in al-Shabaab activities or who have close family members in the group are subject to intense scrutiny from Kenyan security services and often fear retribution from active militants.

Policy Responses to Female Combatants

The presence of female fighters in nonstate armed groups poses a challenge not only for countries facing civil war but for a wide range of countries struggling with violent extremism. How can our analyses inform attempts to counter violent extremism among girls and women? First, consider the multiple paths into and out of armed groups. In some instances personal connections matter a great deal. In Ukraine some women were brought into armed groups because of romantic relationships. Marriages have been a clear pathway into ISIS and al-Shabaab. But across the armed groups we analyze, ideological appeal is a key factor. This is especially so if joining the organization offered an expansion of women's activities beyond what was traditionally acceptable. As a result, no single intervention can address the full range of motivations compelling women to participate in armed conflict. There is no silver bullet to stop female combatants from joining nonstate armed groups any more than there might be for male combatants.

There are, however, issues unique to female fighters that can shed light on what appropriate policy responses might look like. It is clear that some female combatants see their personal security through a gendered lens and as a result willingly choose to join nonstate armed groups. Disruptions in family life and resulting perceptions of vulnerability enable women's participation in multiple contexts. In Ukraine, women feel compelled to join separatist groups when they believe that men are not doing enough to protect their families and communities. Armed groups are seen as offering a kind of alternative family or source of protection for some Colombian women. Tales of FARC women joining to escape domestic abuse and hopelessness should be taken seriously, as should stories of young women joining the PKK to avoid early marriage and gain greater personal agency. The same is true for the concerns of widows and other female heads of households who seek economic opportunities or social support in the arms of a militant group.

When a conflict ends, or when a woman defects from an armed group, she often finds herself doubly stigmatized: first as a compromised or "fallen" woman, and second as a fighter. While women in Colombia have a lower overall recidivism rate than men, they also face distinct reintegration challenges.[36] Some evidence suggests that women may have fought harder on behalf of the FARC and are more loyal to the organization.[37] Data from the Colombian Agency for Reincorporation and Normalization (formerly the Colombian Agency for Reintegration) shows that between 2003 and 2012 just 19.6 percent of individuals who demobilized from the FARC through state-run programs were women.[38] Given that the FARC is believed to be 30 to 40 percent women, this statistic suggests that female fighters are much less likely than men to defect. Compare this also to figures from the demobilization camps established after the 2016 peace accords, which indicate that between 28 and 32 percent of FARC cadres that disarmed were women—a much higher proportion than during the decade in which the government was actively calling on FARC members to defect from the group.[39]

The question of loyalty is relevant in part because it speaks to the social and psychological challenges that female fighters can face during a DDR process. Research on women who demobilized from the Communist Party of Nepal (Maoist) (CPN-M) after the 1996–2006 civil war shows that they struggled with issues of social isolation. Many report feeling rejected by their families and communities, a problem often compounded by the fact that CPN-M leaders encouraged intercaste marriages, widow remarriages, and other unions considered taboo in Nepalese society. Such relationships often dissolved as a result of social pressure after the conflict ended.[40] Losing the labor roles they had within the CPN-M and the social ties they had formed within the ranks likewise led to a loss of identity for some women.[41] Female CPN-M ex-combatants who were shunned by their communities often ended up moving to urban centers, where they once again faced the challenge of rebuilding their lives without close communal ties.[42]

Psychosocial challenges are likewise linked to the economic struggles of demobilized women—a problem not unique to the women of Nepal.[43] Following the defeat of the LTTE in Sri Lanka, female ex-combatants struggled with physical and mental health problems and the difficulties of finding jobs.[44] In Sierra Leone and during earlier DDR efforts in Colombia, women were tracked into low-skilled, low-wage, and gender-stereotyped jobs that did not offer the resources they needed to make a living.[45] In her interviews with former female fighters in El Salvador, Jocelyn Viterna finds that although female guerrillas are more likely to participate in community life after war than women who had not fought, they also are less likely than their noncombatant counterparts to be community leaders.[46] Nearly all of them continue to live in ways dominated by traditional expectations regarding family life and care.

Overall, work on the reintegration of female combatants has highlighted a number of areas for improvement. These include calls to strengthen social networks among ex-combatants, to create job-training opportunities that leverage the skills women gain in combat, and to break down the rigid combatant/noncombatant dichotomy that has historically prevented women involved with nonstate armed groups from participating in DDR programs.[47]

Demobilization in Colombia is now dealing with many of the obstacles previous DDR programs have faced. On a positive note, Colombian women showed up at demobilization sites in far greater numbers than is common after conflicts, and these women have been able to attend the same job training courses as men. Yet there are doubts about the quality of life that awaits them outside the demobilization camps. The UN has expressed concern that reinsertion and reintegration has not been successful, and there have been several violent attacks on ex-guerrillas.[48] Many former FARC cadres—perhaps as many as half—have left demobilization zones to try and make a life on their own, without state support.[49]

While these issues affect all ex-combatants, women face the additional stigma that comes with transgressing gender norms, particularly women from rural and indigenous communities. For example, years of stories about abortion and promiscuity in the FARC has created the perception that Farianas are women of loose morals, even though there are social pressures for them to return to traditional roles as homemakers and caregivers.[50] In fact, with the FARC no longer controlling their fertility, many Farianas become pregnant or give birth at demobilization sites, while others begin looking for the children they were forced to surrender during the war.[51] Still, these are not indications that these women want to hold to traditional roles. Farianas today envision themselves as "insurgent feminists" and look to continue the struggle to upend patriarchy and other forms of oppression through nonviolent means.[52] In a Colombia where the FARC continues to exist as a political party while the ELN and smaller groups continue armed struggle, what are the consequences if DDR programs fail to meet the needs of these women?

Issues relating to demobilization and reintegration affect other contemporary nonstate armed groups as well. Very few of the girls and women who have escaped Boko Haram have been able or allowed to return to their home communities. The few that have done so report severe stigmatization. The Nigerian government has been quick to place women linked to Boko Haram into residential rehabilitation programs where they are kept away from their communities, from their families, and, often, from the children they bore while part of the group. But this approach cuts off from society a group of individuals who are already deeply stigmatized by their association with terrorism, regardless of whether they personally perpetrated attacks or not.

Many countries are also beginning to confront the challenge of dealing with women who supported ISIS. Responses to these women have varied, with some countries dealing out harsh punishments. In Iraq, where hundreds of ISIS women were arrested after the fall of Mosul and other ISIS-held areas, dozens went on trial in early 2018. Some of these have claimed that they were duped into joining ISIS (usually by their husbands or parents) and that they collaborated to survive.[53] By choosing this narrative, women are appealing to one common frame: they are victims of conflict. This tendency to see women as without agency has appeared in the context of many conflicts, and some feminist security studies research has both noted and challenged these assumptions.[54] In the case of ISIS specifically, media coverage has frequently presented the Western women who joined as misguided, forced, or lured into the organization.[55]

While there is evidence that many women who arrived from abroad did come with family members, this does not preclude the possibility that women were also ideologically committed and willing participants. In Iraq, at least, many women have been unsuccessful in their attempts to use being misled as a legal defense. Dozens have been given sentences of death or life in prison, including women from Turkey, Azerbaijan, Russia, and Germany.[56] The pace of the trials (some of which were as short as ten minutes) and a perceived difference in the treatment of Iraqi and non-Iraqi women has sparked some outcry from human rights organizations.[57]

At the same time, it is unclear what a more lenient approach might look like. The United Kingdom has revoked the citizenship of 150 would-be returnees to prevent them from reentering the country.[58] The Canadian government has argued that it must bring home everyone linked to ISIS even though these individuals are unlikely to be convicted in Canadian courts.[59] France has promised that women and their children who wish to return will have their petitions reviewed on a case-by-case basis. In practice, though, the French government has allowed foreign courts to try French nationals and appears to have made little or no proactive effort to have French citizens extradited.[60] Given the number of countries involved, there will almost certainly be a patchwork of policies with respect to returning ISIS supporters, male and female.

The number of women disarming from insurgencies worldwide, combined with the number of women in armed groups that are poised to demobilize sometime in the future, should add urgency to the search for policy solutions. More attention needs to be paid to destigmatizing female fighters and providing extended support for their reintegration. Considerable attention has been devoted to the engagement of women in peace processes, most notably in UN Security Council Resolution 1325 (2000) and related resolutions. The Women, Peace, and Security agenda presumes both that the presence of women enhances the overall success of peace processes and that processes that include women will produce more gender-sensitive agreements. Some empirical research has supported these findings and shown that peace agreements in which women participate as signatories, negotiators, mediators, or witnesses are more durable, more gender-inclusive, and more comprehensive (i.e., they include a broader range of provisions).[61] Yet to date much of the research in this area has concentrated on cases in which women participated in delegations on behalf of state governments or civil society groups. With continued low rates of participation by women in peace talks overall, and with women from nonstate armed groups particularly underrepresented, the few cases in which insurgent women have participated in negotiating teams become crucial case studies.[62] Prior research on some of these cases—in particular, Guatemala and El Salvador—has yielded mixed results. While both of these cases included women in rebel group delegations and both cases successfully resulted in the conclusion of a peace accord, only in Guatemala did the resulting accord address gender issues across a range of provisions.[63] The addition of Colombia to this small group of cases adds additional evidence that the presence of women in insurgent delegations can influence outcomes in a more gender-inclusive way and contribute to success in reaching an accord.

Our findings lend support to the argument that policymakers should devote particular attention to the inclusion of women from nonstate armed groups in peace negotiations. Existing work that is focused on the role of gender in peace negotiations highlights the advantages that rebel women may have over women from civil society groups. Women in civil society, to the extent that they contribute to peace talks at all, are often relegated to the status of what conflict management scholars call Track 3, Track 2, or Track 1.5 actors. Such actors are one or more steps removed from the official Track 1 actors (those engaged in negotiating and decision-making) and they "therefore generally take on a more facilitative, educational, or persuasive role."[64] This creates a complex and highly contextual negotiating environment in which civil society women often rely heavily on proxies, coalition-building, and lobbying to influence peace talks—with mixed results. Examples of this can be found in Kenya, where women saw several of their proposals adopted, but not necessarily as a result of their influence; and in Liberia, where women had to resort to creative tactics like sex strikes, blocking exits to the negotiating rooms, and threatening to strip naked (a shameful act in Liberian society) to pressure male leaders into reaching an accord.[65] By contrast, women in rebel groups may have an advantage in attaining Track 1 status by virtue of their membership in organizations that must be represented at the peace table.

Once at the talks, insurgent women are capable of serving a dual function as representatives of their group and as a conduit for discussion of gender issues. We have seen exactly this dynamic occur in Guatemala, where negotiator Luz Méndez reports that her dialogue with women's organizations as well as with fellow insurgents influenced her contributions to the talks.[66] The often-cited benefits of including women in peace talks generally—and notions that women are more communicative, more creative, better networked, more concerned with a broader range of issues, and possess more specialized knowledge of local contexts and gender issues—can all be extended to rebel women, with the added benefit that women in nonstate armed groups can potentially leverage their legitimacy as Track 1 actors in a post–UN Security Council Resolution 1325 world.[67]

Implications for Scholarship on Insurgent Women

We have sought to add to a growing body of research on the presence and impact of women in nonstate armed groups. In particular we see our findings in dialogue with prior work on the topic in feminist security studies and in international relations more broadly. As other feminist security studies work suggests, our cases show the complex nature of agency and choice as women engage with nonstate armed groups across the ideological spectrum. In particular, the role of familial relationships as both a push factor *and* a pull factor in insurgencies challenges us to think more about gendered agency. Feminist work cautions against the tendency to see women acting only from the frame of wife, mother, or lover, because such conclusions feed into essentialist narratives and ignore the relevance of larger social issues.[68] Read through a feminist lens, the reality that young women join the FARC as a way out of abusive homes tells us something not just about women and abuse; it tells a larger story about a context of poverty, state-sponsored violence against civilians, and national/international economic forces that weigh on and break down traditional family structures.

Additionally, feminist works sheds light on our findings about the variation and fluidity of women's roles in armed conflict. Feminist scholars are skeptical of neat dichotomies like victim/agent or combatant/noncombatant. Such dichotomies often become the foundational point for power dynamics, with feminized concepts (in this case, victims and noncombatants) rendered subjective, dependent, or less visible.[69] Megan MacKenzie finds that in Sierra Leone, women and girls performed both combat and support tasks for armed groups even while gendered logics prioritized their work in support roles and placed them outside the circle of fighters eligible for DDR benefits. Conversely, the fact that men and boys also performed support work was downplayed.[70] This translation of gendered power dynamics into policy may prove a cautionary tale for a place like Ukraine, where the involvement of women as fighters could be overshadowed by their starring roles in propaganda videos. Indeed, the functional importance of a support role like recruiting should not be overlooked in defining who fights.

Turning to work in international relations, we see these cases upholding key findings. Many of the organizations we examine are leftist groups, and several adopt ideologies supportive of gender rights. Our findings align with the results of quantitative studies on the topic.[71] In the case of nationalist/separatist ideologies, we see that in Ukraine and among Kurdish organizations women play a variety of roles in such groups. In the Kurdish case specifically, women's participation is far more extensive among groups that embrace an explicitly leftist and egalitarian ideology. This contrasts with scholarship on African insurgencies and research specific to girl soldiers, which sees a negative relationship between separatism and the presence of female fighters.[72] Yet a regional distinction could be explained by the finding that women are more likely to be incorporated into armed movements overall where they are more educated and therefore constitute a pool of skilled labor.[73]

We also challenge existing work that takes a top-down approach in understanding women's participation in armed groups. Some research in international relations envisions the insurgent organization as a gatekeeper for the recruitment of women. In such a model the group retains control over the decision of whether and in what capacity to admit women and girls based on environmental factors like competition, perceptions of legitimacy, and the need for more recruits.[74] While evidence shows that these factors have some weight, our cases also show that factors at other levels of analysis influence the presence and roles of women.

At the household level, early recruitment efforts by the FARC and ISIS brought entire families into the organization, which meant these organizations had to accept the presence of women—even if they failed to recognize them as "members"—or fear losing male recruits as well. Allowing women was not an explicit policy decision but rather a reality to which the organization had to adapt and respond. At the individual level of analysis, an environment of competition and outbidding can create opportunities for women who aspire to join the fight. We see this in Colombia, where a crowded marketplace of leftist groups allowed women to leave organizations like the ELN when they felt they were being marginalized, and in Turkey, where the PKK's focus on women's liberation expanded from within.

Viewed this way, a competitive environment functions as a two-level game. Groups may force each other to admit women or expand their roles, but women can also use intergroup competition as a strategic opportunity to effect change. The limitations of current quantitative datasets on women in armed groups—which are not fine-grained enough to capture variation in the number of women within an insurgency over its life span—mean that scholars focused on quantitative, cross-national work cannot fully capture or explain the types of change over time that we observe in our cases.

Finally, we consider the relevance of a transorganizational level of analysis. Quantitative work that envisions every nonstate armed group as an independent unit does not fully reflect the dynamics of organizational learning we observed. Insurgencies operating in a competitive environment imitate and learn from each other and from groups in the region or even internationally. Connections between the ELN and Cuba place the ELN within a complicated family tree of Latin American leftist movements; Kurdish groups in Turkey and Syria have a similar relationship. Zooming out further, we find a broader international context from which the ELN's "new left" approach emerged. The new significance of social media and the internet has created a global dialogue between nonstate armed actors as well. At a time when Farianas can correspond online with the women of the PKK, we must take care to acknowledge that global forces as well as factors at the regional, national, and local levels all work to shape the lives of insurgent women.[75]

Notes

1. Reed M. Wood and Jakana L. Thomas, "Women on the Frontline: Rebel Group Ideology and Women's Participation in Violent Rebellion," *Journal of Peace Research* 54, no. 1 (2017): 31–46, doi:10.1177/0022343316675025; Alexis Leanna Henshaw, "Why Women Rebel: Greed, Grievance, and Women in Armed Rebel Groups," *Journal of Global Security Studies* 1, no. 3 (2016): 204–19, doi:10.1093 /jogss/ogw008.

2. "Iran Convicts Sixteen Women for 'Serving ISIS,'" *Radio Farda,* May 7, 2018, https://en.radiofarda.com/a/iran-convicts-16-women-for-serving-is/292 12933.html; "French Female Jihadists Bigger Threat Than Just Housewives: Justice Ministry," *Local,* May 7, 2018, https://www.thelocal.fr/20180507/french -female-jihadists-bigger-threat-than-housewives-justice-ministry/; Taufiq Siddiq, "Fifteen Indonesian Women Arrested in Syria Suspected as ISIS Members," *Tempo English,* February 28, 2018, https://en.tempo.co/read/news/2018/02/28/055 916125/15-Indonesian-Women-Arrested-in-Syria-Suspected-as-ISIS-Members; Shehab Khan, "Hundreds of Foreign Women Who Joined the Islamic State Captured," *Independent,* February 10, 2018, https://www.independent.co.uk/news /world/middle-east/isis-foreign-women-islamic-state-detained-human-rights -watch-a8204686.html.

3. Richard Barrett, *Beyond the Caliphate: Foreign Fighters and the Threat of Returnees* (New York: Soufan Center, 2017), 24–25, http://thesoufancenter.org /research/beyond-caliphate/.

4. Joana Cook and Gina Vale, *From Daesh to "Diaspora": Tracing the Women and Minors of Islamic State* (London: International Centre for the Study of Reconciliation, 2018), 16, https://icsr.info/2018/07/23/from-daesh-to-diaspora -tracing-the-women-and-minors-of-islamic-state/; Behar Xharra and Nita Gojani, *Understanding Push and Pull Factors in Kosovo: Primary Interviews with Returned Foreign Fighters and Their Families* (New York: UN Development Programme, 2017), 16, http://www.ks.undp.org/content/kosovo/en/home/library /democratic_governance/understanding-push-and-pull-factors-in-kosovo —primary-interview.html.

5. Cook and Vale, *From Daesh to "Diaspora,"* 8.

6. Daniel Milton and Brian Dodwell, "Jihadi Brides? Examining a Female Guesthouse Registry from the Islamic State's Caliphate," *Combating Terrorism Center Sentinel* 11, no. 5 (2018): 16–22, https://ctc.usma.edu/jihadi-brides -examining-female-guesthouse-registry-islamic-states-caliphate/.

7. For a discussion of this trope, see Laura Sjoberg, "Jihadi Brides and Female Volunteers: Reading the Islamic State's War to See Gender and Agency in Conflict Dynamics," *Conflict Management and Peace Science* 35, no. 3 (2018): 296–311, doi:10.1177/0738894217695050.

8. Meredith Loken and Anna Zelenz, "Explaining Extremism: Western Women in Daesh," *European Journal of International Security* 3, no. 1 (2017): 67, doi:10.1017/eis.2017.13.

9. For examples, see Raul Dancel, "Philippines Arrests Top Female ISIS Recruiter," *Straits Times,* October 18, 2017, https://www.straitstimes.com/asia /se-asia/philippines-arrest-top-female-isis-recruiter-ex-wife-of-radicalised -singaporean; and Alissa J. Rubin, "She Left France to Fight in Syria. Now She Wants to Return. But Can She?" *New York Times,* January 11, 2018, https://www .nytimes.com/2018/01/11/world/europe/emilie-konig-france-islamic-state.html.

10. Jennifer Philippa Eggert, "Women Fighters in the 'Islamic State' and Al-Qaida in Iraq: A Comparative Analysis," *Journal of International Peace and Organization* 90, nos. 3–4 (2015): 368, http://www.brismes.ac.uk/conference/wp-content/uploads/2017/03/Paper_Eggert_EggertJ.pdf.

11. Umm Sumayyah al-Muhajirah, "Slave Girls or Prostitutes?" *Al Dabiq* 9 (2015): 44–49, https://jihadology.net/2015/05/21/al-%E1%B8%A5ayat-media-center-presents-a-new-issue-of-the-islamic-states-magazine-dabiq-9/.

12. Al-Khansaa Brigade, *Women of the Islamic State: A Manifesto on Women by the Al-Khanssaa Brigade*, trans. Charlie Winter (London: Quilliam, 2015), https://www.quilliaminternational.com/shop/e-publications/women-of-the-islamic-state-a-manifesto-on-women-by-the-al-khanssaa-brigade-2/.

13. Al-Khansaa Brigade, *Women of the Islamic State*; Jacqueline O'Neill, *Engaging Women in Disarmament, Demobilization, and Reintegration: Insights for Colombia* (Washington, DC: Inclusive Security, 2015), https://www.inclusivesecurity.org/wp-content/uploads/2017/01/Policy_Recommendations_Colombia_DDR.pdf.

14. Barrett, *Beyond the Caliphate*, 22–23.

15. Eggert, "Women Fighters," 366.

16. Azadeh Moaveni, "ISIS Women and Enforcers in Syria Recount Collaboration, Anguish, and Escape," *New York Times*, November 21, 2015, https://www.nytimes.com/2015/11/22/world/middleeast/isis-wives-and-enforcers-in-syria-recount-collaboration-anguish-and-escape.html.

17. Loken and Zelenz, "Explaining Extremism," 59n82.

18. Daveed Gartenstein-Ross, Vivian Hagerty, and Logan MacNair, "The Emigrant Sisters Return: The Growing Role of the Islamic State's Women," *War on the Rocks*, April 2, 2018, https://warontherocks.com/2018/04/the-emigrant-sisters-return-the-growing-role-of-the-islamic-states-women/.

19. "Nigeria Chibok Abductions: What We Know," *BBC News*, May 8, 2017, http://www.bbc.com/news/world-africa-32299943; Candi Carter Olson, "#BringBackOurGirls: Digital Communities Supporting Real-World Change and Influencing Mainstream Media Agendas," *Feminist Media Studies* 16, no. 5 (2016): 772–87, doi:10.1080/14680777.2016.1154887; Meredith Loken, "#BringBackOur Girls and the Invisibility of Imperialism," *Feminist Media Studies* 14, no. 6 (2014): 1100–110, doi:10.1080/14680777.2014.975442.

20. Haruna Umar and Sam Olukoya, "Nigeria Government Acknowledges 110 Girls Still Missing," Associated Press, February 25, 2018, https://apnews.com/b09eee70e1304fa2a16e7768cb153593/Nigerian-government-acknowledges-110-girls-still-missing.

21. For a detailed study of women in Boko Haram, see Hilary Matfess, *Women and the War on Boko Haram: Wives, Weapons, Witnesses* (London: Zed, 2017).

22. Jason Warner and Hilary Matfess, *Exploding Stereotypes: The Unexpected Operational and Demographic Characteristics of Boko Haram's Suicide Bombers*

(West Point, NY: Combating Terrorism Center at West Point, 2017), https://ctc
.usma.edu/report-exploding-stereotypes-the-unexpected-operational-and
-demographic-characteristics-of-boko-harams-suicide-bombers/.

23. Warner and Matfess, *Exploding Stereotypes*, 24.

24. "Four Killed in Multiple Suicide Blasts in Maiduguri," *Guardian*, May 4,
2018, https://t.guardian.ng/news/four-killed-in-multiple-suicide-blasts-in
-maiduguri/.

25. Mia Bloom, *Bombshell: Women and Terrorism* (Philadelphia: University
of Pennsylvania Press, 2011).

26. Hassan Mwakimako, "Coastal Muslim Women in the Coast of Kenya:
Narrating Radicalization, Gender, Violence and Extremism," *African Review* 45,
no. 1 (2018): 49–69, http://journals.udsm.ac.tz/index.php/ar/article/view/1663.

27. Diana Wanyonyi, "Escape from al-Shabab: 'I Was Turned into a Sex
Slave,'" Deutsche Welle, March 3, 2018, http://www.dw.com/en/escape-from-al
-shabab-i-was-turned-into-a-sex-slave/a-42762342; Charlotte Attwood, "The Sex
Slaves of al-Shabab," *BBC News,* May 25, 2017, http://www.bbc.com/news/maga
zine-40022953.

28. Irene Ndung'u, Uyo Salifu, and Romi Sigsworth, *Violent Extremism in
Kenya: Why Women Are a Priority* (Pretoria, South Africa: Institute for Security
Studies, 2017), 39, https://issafrica.org/research/monographs/violent-extremism
-in-kenya-why-women-are-a-priority.

29. Fatuma A. Ali, "Understanding the Role of Gender Relations in Recruiting
Young Muslim Women in Higher Learning Institutions in Kenya," *African Review*
45, no. 1 (2018): 70–95, http://journals.udsm.ac.tz/index.php/ar/article/view/1664.

30. Ndung'u, Salifu, and Sigsworth, *Violent Extremism in Kenya,* 39.

31. Cassidy Parker, *Commanding Attention: A Female Al-Shabaab Ex-
Commander Speaks Out* (Pretoria, South Africa: Institute for Security Studies,
2017), https://issafrica.org/iss-today/commanding-attention-a-female-al-shabaab
-ex-commander-speaks-out.

32. Joseph Akwiri, "Robed Women Petrol-Bomb Police Station in Menya's
Mombasa," Reuters, September 11, 2016, https://www.reuters.com/article/us
-kenya-attacks/robed-women-petrol-bomb-police-station-in-kenyas-mombasa
-idUSKCN11H0AC.

33. Jason Warner and Ellen Chapin, *Targeted Terror: The Suicide Bombers of
al-Shabaab* (West Point, NY: Combating Terrorism Center at West Point, 2018),
22–24, https://ctc.usma.edu/targeted-terror-suicide-bombers-al-shabaab/.

34. US Department of Justice, "Three Defendants Arrested on Charges of
Providing Material Support to a Foreign Terrorist Organization," news release,
July 23, 2014, https://www.fbi.gov/contact-us/field-offices/washingtondc/news
/press-releases/three-defendants-arrested-on-charges-of-providing-material
-support-to-a-foreign-terrorist-organization.

35. Fathima A. Badurdeen, "Women and Recruitment in the Al-Shabaab Network: Stories of Women Being Recruited by Women Recruiters in the Coastal Region of Kenya," *African Review* 45, no. 1 (2018): 19–48, http://journals.udsm.ac.tz/index.php/ar/article/view/1662.

36. Oliver Kaplan and Enzo Nussio, "Explaining Recidivism of Ex-Combatants in Colombia," *Journal of Conflict Resolution* 62, no. 1 (2018): 64–93, doi:/10.1177/0022002716644326. Recidivism here is defined as a return to any illegal activity, including gang violence and drug trafficking/cultivation as well as a return to an armed group.

37. Natalia Herrera and Douglas Porch, "'Like Going to a Fiesta'—The Role of Female Fighters in Colombia's FARC-EP," *Small Wars and Insurgencies* 19, no. 4 (2008): 609–34, doi:10.1080/09592310802462547.

38. Laura Linero and Carlos Morels, "Las Cifras de Los 10 Años de Desmovilizaciones" (Figures from ten years of demobilizations), *El Tiempo*, accessed August 29, 2018, http://www.eltiempo.com/Multimedia/especiales/desmovilizados/ARCHIVO/ARCHIVO-12224321-0.pdf.

39. Natalio Cosoy, "6.900 Guerrilleros de Las FARC Ya Están Concentrados En 26 Zonas En Colombia . . . ¿Y Qué Sigue Ahora?" (Sixty-nine hundred FARC guerrillas are now concentrated in twenty-six zones in Colombia . . . What happens next?), *BBC Mundo*, February 22, 2017, http://www.bbc.com/mundo/noticias-america-latina-38888897; Redacción El Tiempo, "Cerca de 1.800 Guerrilleras de las Farc Irán a Sitios de Desarme" (Close to eighteen hundred FARC guerrillas going to disarmament sites), *El Tiempo*, February 4, 2017, http://www.eltiempo.com/politica/proceso-de-paz/cifra-de-guerrilleras-de-las-farc-que-iran-a-zonas-de-concentracion-49116.

40. Roshimi Goswami, *UNSCR 1325 and Female Ex-Combatants: Case Study of the Maoist Women of Nepal* (New York: UN Women, 2015), http://www.unwomen.org/en/digital-library/publications/2017/5/unscr-1325-and-female-ex-combatants; Amrita Pritam Gogoi, "Troubled Identities: Women Ex-Combatants in Post-Conflict Nepal," in *Women, Peace, and Security in Nepal: From Civil War to Post-Conflict Reconstruction*, ed. Åshild Kolås (Abingdon, UK: Routledge, 2017), 50–65; Lorina Sthapit and Philippe Doneys, "Female Maoist Combatants during and after the People's War," in *Women, Peace, and Security in Nepal: From Civil War to Post-Conflict Reconstruction*, ed. Åshild Kolås (Abingdon, UK: Routledge, 2017), 33–49.

41. Gogoi, "Troubled Identities."

42. Goswami, *UNSCR 1325 and Female Ex-Combatants*.

43. Indeed, such problems are also not unique to female veterans of nonstate armed groups. See, among others, Gayle Tzemach Lemmon, *Ashley's War: The Untold Story of a Team of Women Soldiers on the Special Ops Battlefield* (New York: Harper, 2015), on the sense of isolation and lack of opportunity among

returned veterans of US military Female and Cultural Engagement Teams in Afghanistan.

44. Rebecca Murray, "Scarred by Sri Lanka's War with Tamil Tigers, Female Ex-Fighters Build New Lives," *Christian Science Monitor,* October 9, 2010, https://www.csmonitor.com/World/Asia-South-Central/2010/1029/Scarred-by-Sri-Lanka-s-war-with-Tamil-Tigers-female-ex-fighters-build-new-lives; Holly Robertson, "From Soldiers to Housewives: Women Who Fought as Tamil Tigers in Sri Lanka Are Forced into Traditional Roles," *Washington Post,* June 7, 2018, https://www.washingtonpost.com/world/asia_pacific/the-women-who-fought-for-the-tamil-tigers-in-sri-lanka-are-being-forced-into-traditional-roles/2018/06/06/6894df7a-681a-11e8-bea7-c8eb28bc52b1_story.html?utm_term=.af5f7745c4ad.

45. Megan H. MacKenzie, *Female Soldiers in Sierra Leone: Sex, Security, and Post-Conflict Development* (New York: New York University Press, 2012); Megan Alpert, "To Be a Guerrilla, and a Woman, in Colombia," *Atlantic,* September 28, 2016, https://www.theatlantic.com/international/archive/2016/09/farc-deal-female-fighters/501644/.

46. Jocelyn Viterna, *Women in War: The Micro-Processes of Mobilization in El Salvador* (Oxford: Oxford University Press, 2013), 204.

47. Dyan E. Mazurana and Linda Eckerbom Cole, "Women, Girls, and Disarmament, Demobilization and Reintegration (DDR)," in *Women and Wars: Contested Histories, Uncertain Futures,* ed. Carol Cohn (Malden, MA: Polity, 2013), 194–214; O'Neill, *Engaging Women in Disarmament*; Megan H. MacKenzie and Christopher Hills, "Women in Non-State Armed Groups after War: The (Non)Evolution of Disarmament, Demobilization, and Reintegration," in *The Palgrave International Handbook of Gender and the Military,* ed. Rachel Woodward and Claire Duncanson (London: Palgrave Macmillan, 2017), 455–74; Alexis Leanna Henshaw, "Female Combatants in Post-Conflict Processes: Understanding the Roots of Exclusion," *Journal of Global Security Studies* (forthcoming).

48. Sara Reardon, "Colombia: After the Violence," *Nature News,* 2018, https://www.nature.com/immersive/d41586-018-04976-7/index.html; Edith M. Lederer, "UN Official: Reintegrating Colombia Rebels Is Not Going Well," *Chicago Tribune,* October 21, 2017, http://www.chicagotribune.com/sns-bc-un—united-nations-colombia-20171020-story.html.

49. Reardon, "Colombia."

50. Sruthi Gottipati, "Colombia's Female FARC Fighters Wage a New War, for Gender Parity," *IRIN,* September 7, 2017, https://www.irinnews.org/feature/2017/09/07/colombia-s-female-farc-fighters-wage-new-war-gender-parity; Camille Boutron and Diana Gómez, "From Rifles to Aprons? The Challenges of Reincorporating Colombia's Female Ex-Combatants into Civilian and Political Life," *LSE Latin America and Caribbean* blog, March 8, 2017, http://blogs.lse.ac

.uk/latamcaribbean/2017/03/08/from-rifles-to-aprons-the-challenges-of
-reincorporating-colombias-female-ex-combatants-into-civilian-and-political
-life/.

51. Margarita Rodriguez, "Colombia's Rebel Mothers Seeking Lost Children,"
BBC News, August 5, 2014, http://www.bbc.com/news/magazine-28600850; Emily
Wright, "The End of FARC's Fifty-Year Pregnancy Ban Leads to a Baby Boom,"
Public Radio International, July 20, 2017, https://www.pri.org/stories/2017-07-20
/end-farcs-50-year-pregnancy-ban-leads-baby-boom.

52. Alexandra Phelan, "Insurgent Feminism and Colombia's New Peace,"
Monash Gender, Peace and Security blog, July 26, 2017, http://www.monashgps
.org/single-post/2017/07/27/Insurgent-Feminism-and-Colombias-New-Peace.

53. Martin Chulov and Nadia al-Faour, "'They Deserve No Mercy': Iraq Deals
Briskly with Accused 'Women of ISIS,'" *Guardian*, May 22, 2018, http://www
.theguardian.com/world/2018/may/22/they-deserve-no-mercy-iraq-deals
-briskly-with-accused-women-of-isis; "Iraq: Nineteen Russian Women Handed
Life Sentences for Joining ISIL," Al Jazeera, April 29, 2018, https://www.aljazeera
.com/news/2018/04/iraq-19-russian-women-handed-life-sentences-joining
-isil-180429143235839.html; "Twelve ISIL Widows Sentenced to Death, Life by
Iraqi Court," Al Jazeera, February 18, 2018, https://www.aljazeera.com/news
/2018/02/12-isil-widows-sentenced-death-life-iraqi-court-180218172230088.html.

54. Sjoberg, "Jihadi Brides and Female Volunteers"; Alexis Leanna Henshaw,
Why Women Rebel: Understanding Women's Participation in Armed Rebel Groups
(London: Routledge, 2017); Alexis Leanna Henshaw, "Where Women Rebel: Pat-
terns of Women's Participation in Armed Rebel Groups 1990–2008," *Interna-
tional Feminist Journal of Politics* 18, no. 1 (2016): 39–60, doi:10.1080/14616742
.2015.1007729; Laura Sjoberg and Caron E. Gentry, *Mothers, Monsters, Whores:
Women's Violence in Global Politics*, 2nd ed. (London: Zed, 2016); Megan H.
MacKenzie, *Female Soldiers in Sierra Leone*.

55. Sjoberg, "Jihadi Brides and Female Volunteers."

56. Chulov and al-Faour, "They Deserve No Mercy"; "Iraq: Nineteen Russian
Women"; "Twelve ISIL Widows Sentenced."

57. Belkis Wille, "Unfair ISIS Trial in Iraq Hands Women Harshest Sentences,"
Human Rights Watch, February 21, 2018, https://www.hrw.org/news/2018/02/21
/unfair-isis-trial-iraq-hands-women-harshest-sentences.

58. Estimates for the potential use of exclusion powers in the United Kingdom
range from two hundred to three hundred persons. Fiona Hamilton, "Two Hundred ISIS Fighters Who Came from UK Cannot Return," *Times*, February 17,
2018, https://www.thetimes.co.uk/article/200-isis-fighters-who-came-from-uk
-cannot-return-wrg8lvpjd; "UK 'Has Stripped 150 Jihadists and Criminals of
Citizenship,'" *Guardian*, July 30, 2017, https://www.theguardian.com/uk-news
/2017/jul/30/uk-has-stripped-150-jihadists-and-criminals-of-citizenship.

59. Stewart Bell, "Exclusive: Canada's Plan for Managing the Return of ISIS Fighters Revealed in Documents," *Global News*, May 14, 2018, https://globalnews .ca/news/4205480/canadas-plan-freturn-isis-fighters/.

60. Rubin, "She Left France."

61. Jana Krause, Werner Krause, and Piia Bränfors, "Women's Participation in Peace Negotiations and the Durability of Peace," *International Interactions* (forthcoming), accessed August 29, 2018, doi: 10.1080/03050629.2018.1492386; Patty Chang, Mayesha Alam, Roslyn Warren, Rukmani Bhatia, and Rebecca Turkington, *Women Leading Peace* (Washington, DC: Georgetown Institute for Women, Peace, and Security, 2015), https://giwps.georgetown.edu/resource /women-leading-peace/; Sanam Naraghi Anderlini, *Women at the Peace Table: Making a Difference* (New York: UN Women, 2000), http://www.unwomen.org /en/digital-library/publications/2000/1/women-at-the-peace-table-making-a -difference.

62. *Women's Participation in Peace Negotiations: Connections between Presence and Influence*, 2nd ed. (New York: UN Women, 2012), http://www.peace women.org/node/92120.

63. Krause et al., "Women's Participation in Peace Negotiations"; Chang et al., "Women Leading Peace."

64. Diana Chagas, "Capacities and Limits of NGOs as Conflict Managers," in *Leashing the Dogs of War: Conflict Management in a Divided World*, ed. Chester Crocker, Fen Osler Hampson, and Pamela Aall (Washington, DC: US Institute of Peace, 2007), 477–96.

65. Chang et al., "Women Leading Peace," 71–96; Lleymah Gbowee and Carol Mithers, *Mighty Be Our Powers: How Sisterhood, Prayer, and Sex Changed a Nation at War* (New York: Beast, 2011); *Pray the Devil Back to Hell*, directed by Gini Reticker (New York: Fork Films, 2008).

66. Malathi de Alwis, Julie Mertus, and Tazreena Sajjad, "Women and Peace Processes," in *Women and Wars*, ed. Carol Cohn (Malden, MA: Polity, 2013), 169–93.

67. Krause et al., "Women's Participation in Peace Negotiations"; de Alwis et al., "Women and Peace Processes"; Mark A. Boyer, Brian Urlacher, Natalie Florea Hudson, Anat Niv-Solomon, Laura L. Janik, Michael J. Butler, Scott W. Brown, and Andri Ioannou, "Gender and Negotiation: Some Experimental Findings from an International Negotiation Simulation," *International Studies Quarterly* 53, no. 1 (2009): 23–47, doi:10.1111/j.1468–2478.2008.01522.x; Natalie B. Florea, Mark A. Boyer, Michael J. Butler, Scott W. Brown, Magnolia Hernandez, Kimberly Weir, Lin Meng, Paula R. Johnson, Clarisse Lima, and Hayley J. Mayall, "Negotiating from Mars to Venus: Gender in Simulated International Negotiations," *Simulation and Gaming* 34, no. 2 (2003): 226–48, doi:10.1177/1046878103034002005.

68. Sjoberg and Gentry, *Mothers, Monsters, Whores*, chap. 4.

69. Anne Sisson Runyan and V. Spike Peterson, *Global Gender Issues in the New Millennium*, 4th ed. (Boulder, CO: Westview, 2013), 46–47.

70. MacKenzie, *Female Soldiers in Sierra Leone*, 45–62.

71. Wood and Thomas, "Women on the Frontline"; Henshaw, *Why Women Rebel*; Henshaw, "Why Women Rebel,"; Jakana L. Thomas and Kanisha Bond, "Women's Participation in Violent Political Organizations," *American Political Science Review* 109, no. 3 (2015): 488–506, doi:10.1017/S0003055415000313.

72. Thomas and Bond, "Women's Participation"; Roos Haer and Tobias Böhmelt, "Girl Soldiering in Rebel Groups, 1989–2013: Introducing a New Dataset," *Journal of Peace Research* 55, no. 3 (2018): 395–403, doi:10.1177/0022343317752540.

73. Wood and Thomas, "Women on the Frontline."

74. Thomas and Bond, "Women's Participation"; Haer and Böhmelt, "Girl Soldiering in Rebel Groups."

75. Women of the FARC-EP Peace Delegation, "Respuesta a Carta Del PKK" (Response to the PKK's letter), *CeDeMA*, December 22, 2012, http://cedema.org/ver.php?id=5365.

About the Authors

ALEXIS HENSHAW is assistant professor at Troy University. She is the author of *Why Women Rebel: Understanding Women's Participation in Armed Rebel Groups* (Routledge, 2017). Her research has appeared in *Journal of Global Security Studies, International Feminist Journal of Politics, Sexuality and Culture,* and a variety of other peer-reviewed outlets. Henshaw has also written for *The Conversation* and *The Monkey Cage,* the political blog of the *Washington Post.* She received her PhD in political science with a certificate in gender and women's studies from the University of Arizona and previously taught at Duke University and Miami University.

ORA SZEKELY is associate professor in the Department of Political Science at Clark University, where she is also affiliated with the programs Peace Studies and Women's and Gender Studies. Szekely is the author of *The Politics of Militant Group Survival in the Middle East: Resources, Relationships, and Resistance* (Palgrave Macmillan, 2017). Her research has appeared in *Middle East Policy, Foreign Policy Analysis, Studies in Conflict and Terrorism,* and the *Journal of Peace Research,* among other journals, as well as in other publications such as *Lawfare* and *The Monkey Cage.* She has conducted field research in Turkey, Jordan, Syria, Lebanon, Israel, Palestine, Germany, and Egypt. Szekely holds a PhD in political science from McGill University.

JESSICA TRISKO DARDEN is assistant professor at American University's School of International Service. She has been Jeane Kirkpatrick Fellow at the American Enterprise Institute, visiting scholar at Yale University's Program on Order, Conflict, and Violence, and teaching fellow at Yale's Jackson Institute for Global Affairs. Trisko Darden is the author of *Aiding and Abetting: US Foreign Assistance and State Violence* (Stanford, 2019). She has published in peer-reviewed journals and in a range of media outlets including *The Conversation, The Guardian, The Hill, Newsweek, War on the Rocks*, and the *Washington Post*. Trisko Darden holds a PhD in political science from McGill University and an MA in Russian, East European, and Eurasian studies from the University of Texas at Austin.

CPSIA information can be obtained
at www.ICGtesting.com
Printed in the USA
BVHW030503241218
536044BV00004B/11/P